THE ULTIMATE

CROCK POT COOKBOOK FOR

Busy People

+1800 Days of Wholesome, healthy, and Family-Friendly Recipes For Beginners | Super Tasty Dishes Inspired By Global Cuisine Included.

LUISA JOHNSON

TABLE OF CONTENTS

CHAPTER 1: INTRODUCTION AND STORIES

- **Introduction**

Welcome to "The Ultimate Crockpot Cookbook for Busy People." This cookbook is your gateway to a world of culinary convenience, global flavors, and the joy of effortless home cooking. We invite you to embark on a journey that celebrates the art of slow cooking and the rich tapestry of dishes that can be created with your trusty Crockpot, your miracle device that will save you a lot of time.

In our fast-paced lives, finding time to prepare delicious, homemade meals can be a challenge. The daily hustle often leaves us yearning for the comfort of a home-cooked dish but struggling to find the time and energy to make it happen. This is where the Crockpot steps in as your culinary savior, a versatile and reliable kitchen companion that improves even the busiest of days while still giving you great culinary experiences.

A Culinary Adventure Awaits

Our cookbook is more than just a collection of recipes; it's a culinary adventure that spans the globe. We have taken inspiration from different culinary traditions and combined them with the ease and versatility of Crockpot cooking. As you flip through these pages, you'll discover a diverse array of flavors, ingredients, and cooking techniques. From hearty stews to exotic curries, this cookbook offers a wide range of recipes designed to cater to your palate and lifestyle.

The Crockpot: Your Culinary Partner

Before we dive into the recipes, it's essential to understand that the Crockpot isn't just an appliance; it's your culinary partner. We'll guide you through choosing the perfect Crockpot for your needs, equipping your kitchen with essential tools, and caring for your appliance to ensure its longevity.

With the Crockpot by your side, you'll be able to create mouthwatering dishes without the stress of traditional cooking methods. It empowers you to craft gourmet-quality meals with minimal effort, whether you're a seasoned chef or a kitchen novice.

A Cookbook for Everyone

We understand that your life is unique, and so are your culinary preferences. That's why this cookbook is designed to cater to a diverse audience. Whether you're a busy professional, a student, a homemaker, or someone who simply appreciates the convenience of slow cooking, you'll find recipes that suit your needs.

We've included options for vegetarians, meat lovers, and those with a sweet tooth. The Crockpot's versatility allows you to create a wide range of dishes, and we've ensured that there's something here for everyone.

Unlock the Full Potential

As you navigate through this cookbook, we invite you to immerse yourself in the world of Crockpot cooking, experiment with flavors, and share the joy of delicious meals with your loved ones. Each recipe is an opportunity to connect with the art of slow cooking, and the stories you create around your dining table are an integral part of this culinary journey.

Begin Your Journey

Your culinary adventure begins with the turn of a page, the selection of a recipe, and the excitement of creation. We're thrilled to be your companions on this gastronomic exploration. We invite you to read this cookbook as you wish, even jumping from recipe to recipe, be inspired, to absorb the knowledge and immerse yourself in the culinary experiences it offers.

The Crockpot has the power to surprise you with its versatility, and you may discover new favorites that become staples in your home.

How to Make the Most of This Cookbook

To make the most of this cookbook, we recommend a few simple but effective strategies:

- **Plan Your Meals:** Take a moment to look through the recipes and plan your meals for the week. This can save you time, effort, and ensure you have all the ingredients you need.
- **Experiment and Adapt:** Don't be afraid to experiment with the recipes. If you have dietary restrictions or personal preferences, feel free to adapt the recipes to suit your needs.
- **Share Your Creations:** The joy of cooking is often best experienced when shared with others. Invite friends and family to enjoy your Crockpot creations and savor the memories you create around the dining table.

With these strategies in mind, you're ready to embark on a journey that combines the convenience of slow cooking with the excitement of global flavors. Your adventure starts here, and we're thrilled to be your companions as you explore the culinary magic of the Crockpot. Enjoy the journey!

- **A Taste of Stories: Engaging Dining Anecdotes**

In a cozy corner of a dimly lit bistro, a gentle murmur of conversations enveloped the room. The scent of simmering dishes wafted through the air, teasing the senses and promising a delightful evening. This is where our journey begins, with a collection of dining anecdotes that have weaved themselves into the fabric of the culinary world.

Picture a romantic date night, where the flicker of candlelight casts dancing shadows on the table. As the first spoonful of a hearty beef stew finds its way to the diner's lips, memories are made. The laughter, the tender glances, and the whispered sweet nothings blend with the flavors, creating a cherished experience that lingers for a lifetime.

From the bustling streets of New Orleans to the serene landscapes of Tuscany, our stories traverse the globe, capturing the essence of unforgettable dining moments. There's the tale of a family reunion where generations come together over a slow-cooked pot roast, sharing secrets and traditions. And then, the heartwarming account of a cozy winter evening, wrapped in the aroma of chicken soup, where friends found warmth in both the dish and each other's company.

These dining anecdotes aren't just stories; they're a testament to the power of food to connect us, to create lasting memories, and to bring joy to the most ordinary or extraordinary occasions. As we delve into the world of Crockpot cooking, these stories serve as a reminder that it's not just about the recipes; it's about the experiences and connections they foster.

So, pull up a chair, savor the flavors, and let these dining tales whisk you away to the heart of culinary delight. In each story, you'll find a piece of your own culinary journey, a reminder that food is the thread that binds us all.

Here are a couple of engaging dining anecdotes for your section, "A Taste of Stories: Engaging Dining Anecdotes":

Story 1: The Serendipitous Sunday Roast

On a crisp Sunday morning, as the sun lazily climbed the sky, Sarah found herself in a culinary predicament. Her friends had spontaneously decided to visit her for lunch, and her pantry was less than inspiring. With a limited selection of ingredients, she decided to try her hand at a classic pot roast recipe she'd found in her grandmother's old cookbook.

As the pot roast simmered in the Crockpot, the aroma filled the house, and the anticipation grew. When her friends arrived, they were met with an aroma that transported them back to their childhoods. Laughter and conversation flowed as the tender meat practically melted in their mouths. The Crockpot had worked its magic, turning a simple Sunday into an unforgettable gathering of friends, making cherished memories out of unexpected circumstances.

Story 2: The Parisian Affair

Marie and John had always dreamt of a romantic getaway to Paris. They finally managed to make it a reality, and their evenings were filled with candlelit dinners at charming bistros. On one particularly enchanting evening, they found themselves at a tiny, family-owned restaurant hidden away in a cobblestone alley.

The meal was exquisite, with every dish carefully prepared to perfection. But what truly stole their hearts was the slow-cooked coq au vin, served in an heirloom crockpot. The dish was rich and bursting with flavor, and they savored every bite. The owners of the restaurant shared the history of the crockpot, passed down through generations, and how it had become an integral part of their family's culinary heritage.

As they savored the last morsels of coq au vin, Marie and John felt an overwhelming sense of connection, not only to each other but to the long history of passionate chefs who had perfected their craft over the years. This dining experience in the heart of Paris became a memory they would treasure forever.

These stories capture the essence of shared moments and culinary discoveries that make dining a truly remarkable experience. They remind us that the Crockpot is not just a kitchen appliance; it's a vessel for creating lasting memories and connections through the love of food.

- **Authors Culinary Journey**

Before I share the secrets and recipes that have filled the pages of this Crockpot cookbook, I want to take you on a journey—a journey into my own culinary world.

My love affair with cooking began long before I donned the chef's hat or wielded a ladle in the kitchen. It was born from cherished childhood memories of my grandmother's kitchen, where I would watch in awe as she effortlessly transformed simple ingredients into culinary masterpieces. Her ancient, well-worn crockpot was her trusted companion, and it held the promise of heartwarming meals that brought our family together.

As I grew older, the allure of the kitchen remained a constant in my life. I embarked on my own culinary adventures, experimenting with recipes, and developing a deep appreciation for the slow and steady art of Crockpot cooking. The soothing rhythm of chopping, sautéing, and patiently waiting for the flavors to meld into a harmonious symphony became my sanctuary.

Through the years, I encountered countless challenges, from culinary mishaps to the euphoria of successfully recreating a beloved family recipe. Each experience, whether triumphant or humbling, contributed to my journey as a home cook and a passionate advocate for Crockpot cuisine.

In this cookbook, you will find the culmination of my culinary odyssey—a collection of recipes that have been tried, tested, and savored. These dishes represent not just meals but milestones in my life, each with its own story and significance.

I invite you to embark on this culinary adventure with me. Just as my journey has led me here, your exploration of these recipes will be a journey of taste, tradition, and togetherness.

Welcome to my kitchen, where the magic of Crockpot cooking awaits you.

- **The Essence of Crockpot Success**

Picture this: a cold, blustery day outside, and you, snug and warm inside, with the rich aroma of a simmering stew enveloping your home. The essence of Crockpot success is the anticipation of that moment, the knowledge that while you go about your daily routine, a masterpiece is being crafted in your kitchen.

It starts with the ingredients—the freshest produce, the choicest cuts of meat, and the perfect blend of seasonings. The essence of Crockpot success is the art of selection, the knowledge of what will infuse your dish with the flavors you desire.

Temperature control is paramount. The essence of Crockpot success is the steady, gentle heat that allows the ingredients to release their essence, slowly building a symphony of flavors. It's the tender, fall-apart texture that defines a perfectly cooked Crockpot creation.

Patience is your most valuable ally. The essence of Crockpot success is the understanding that great things take time. It's the ability to walk away from the kitchen and trust that your slow cooker is working its magic, infusing every bite with layers of flavor.

CHAPTER 2: THE WORLD OF CROCKPOTS

- **What Is a Crockpot?**

In the world of culinary gadgets, the Crockpot, stands as an unassuming hero—a reliable companion that simplifies the art of cooking while delivering a symphony of flavors. It has earned its place in kitchens across the globe, becoming an essential tool for those who appreciate the beauty of convenience, patience, and the unparalleled taste of slow-cooked dishes.

Crockpot is a versatile electric cooking device At its core, a Crockpot is a versatile electric cooking device created and patented by an inventor named Irving Naxon as a pot exclusively for cooking beans. After little success, the inventor sold the patent to Rival Manifacturing, a Kansas City company. Released into the market under the name Crock Pot and introduced as a slow cooker capable of cooking everything, this appliance has earned its place in kitchens around the world as an essential time-saving tool that will save busy housewives and workers.

The true magic of a Crockpot lies in its heating element, adjustable with settings such as high, low, and sometimes a "keep warm" option, provides a consistent source of heat to the pot's contents. This gradual, uniform cooking method helps even the toughest cuts of meat become tender, rendering them succulent and melt-in-your-mouth delicious. It's a culinary alchemy that extracts the essence of each ingredient, combining them into harmonious, flavorful creations.

Crockpots are available in various sizes, allowing you to choose the one that best suits your needs, whether you're preparing a family feast or a cozy dinner for two. The choice of pot material can also impact your cooking experience. Ceramic pots are known for their even heat distribution, while inox (stainless steel) pots are durable and may offer a different cooking experience.

Perhaps one of the most compelling features of a Crockpot is its "set-it-and-forget-it" convenience. Once your carefully selected ingredients are in the pot, you can leave them to simmer, meld, and transform while you attend to other daily activities. There's no need for constant stirring or monitoring. The Crockpot takes the reins, ensuring your meal reaches its peak of flavor.

Over the hours, a Crockpot fills your home with the tantalizing aroma of a hearty stew, a fragrant curry, or a savory chili, creating a sense of anticipation that is as much a part of the experience as the final meal itself. It's a promise of a delicious dinner with minimal effort, making it a favorite tool for busy families and individuals.

- **Crockpot vs. Slow Cooker: Unveiling the Differences**

In the world of convenient and hands-off cooking, the terms "Crockpot" and "slow cooker" are often used interchangeably. They both offer the allure of effortless meal preparation and the tantalizing promise of returning to a perfectly cooked dish at the end of a busy day. However, while they share the same goal—to make cooking easier and more flavorful—their differences lie in the details.

Temperature Control: One key difference lies in the way they control temperature. Crockpots, as a brand, traditionally have two settings: "high" and "low." These settings provide a relatively simple way to control cooking temperature. In contrast, generic slow cookers often have a broader range of temperature settings, allowing for more precise control.

Design and Shape: Crockpots typically have an oval or round shape, which some cooks find more suitable for specific dishes. In contrast, slow cookers come in various shapes, including oval, round, and rectangular, offering more versatility when it comes to accommodating different recipes.

Cooking Time: Another aspect where these appliances differ is cooking time. Crockpots, being straightforward in their design, often cook at a slightly higher temperature, which can result in shorter cooking times. Slow cookers may offer more flexibility, with longer cooking times for recipes that require it.

Lid Design: Crockpot lids are typically made of glass and come with a tight seal, which helps retain moisture and heat. In comparison, slow cooker lids may vary in design and materials, which can affect the cooking process and the release of steam.

Heating Element: In slow cookers, some dishes may burn or stick to the bottom if not stirred, due to the placement of the heating element at the bottom of the pot. That's why for those who plan to prepare food primarily away from home or overnight, choosing a Crockpot may be the most appropiate. In fact, the heating element in crock pots is located all around the pot, and this difference allows for more even heat distribution, eliminating the need for stirring.

Brand-Specific Features: Crockpots, as a brand, often come with unique features such as digital timers, delay start functions, and more. These features can add convenience to your cooking process. Generic slow cookers also offer a range of features, but the specific options may vary from one model to another.

Despite these differences, both Crockpots and slow cookers excel at creating delicious, slow-cooked meals with minimal effort. Your choice between the two may come down to personal preferences, available features, and the specific needs of your recipes.

In this cookbook, we'll explore recipes that can be prepared in either a Crockpot or a slow cooker, so you can enjoy the delightful flavors of slow-cooked dishes regardless of your appliance choice. As we unveil the distinctions between these kitchen companions, remember that both are capable of transforming ordinary ingredients into extraordinary meals, enriching your culinary journey with ease and flavor.

- **Crockpot vs. Instant Pot: A Quick Comparison**

In the realm of kitchen appliances, two names frequently surface in conversations about efficient and time-saving cooking: the "Crockpot" and the "Instant Pot." Both have their dedicated fan bases, and while they share the objective of simplifying meal preparation, they do so in distinctive ways. Let's explore the differences between these two culinary workhorses.

Cooking Speed:

• **Crockpot:** True to its name, a Crockpot is designed for slow and steady cooking. It operates at a low and consistent temperature, making it perfect for simmering, stewing, and braising dishes over an extended period. The hallmark of a Crockpot is its ability to transform tough cuts of meat into tender, succulent meals through hours of gentle cooking.

• **Instant Pot:** In contrast, an Instant Pot is all about speed. It's a multifunctional appliance that combines various cooking methods, such as pressure cooking, slow cooking, sautéing, and more. While it can replicate the slow-cooking aspect of a Crockpot, an Instant Pot's primary claim to fame is its ability to drastically reduce cooking time, especially for recipes that traditionally take hours.

Versatility:

• **Crockpot:** Crockpots are designed primarily for slow cooking, and that's where they excel. They are perfect for dishes that benefit from long, slow simmering, like stews, soups, and pot roasts. While they can handle certain variations, their true strength lies in the slow-cooking domain.

• **Instant Pot:** The Instant Pot, on the other hand, is a versatile kitchen workhorse. It can be a pressure cooker, slow cooker, rice cooker, steamer, and more. If you're looking for an appliance that can quickly whip up a variety of meals, the Instant Pot is a top contender. It's known for its ability to reduce cooking times, making it ideal for busy individuals and families.

Ease of Use:

• **Crockpot:** Crockpots are known for their simplicity. You can add your ingredients, set the temperature, and let it work its magic. The process is straightforward and doesn't require much monitoring.

• **Instant Pot:** While versatile, Instant Pots may have a steeper learning curve due to their many functions and settings. However, once you're familiar with how it operates, it offers an array of cooking options at your fingertips.

Meal Variety:

• **Crockpot:** Crockpots excel at creating hearty, slow-cooked dishes like chili, pot roast, and pulled pork. They're fantastic for meals that benefit from hours of simmering.

• **Instant Pot:** Instant Pots are well-suited for a wide range of recipes, from quick pasta dishes to braised meats. They can expand your culinary repertoire with their ability to pressure cook, sauté, and perform other functions.

Your choice between a Crockpot and an Instant Pot depends on your cooking style, your need for speed, and the variety of meals you enjoy preparing. Both appliances offer valuable contributions to the kitchen, and in this cookbook, you'll find recipes tailored to both, allowing you to savor the unique advantages of each, depending on your preferences and time constraints.

• **Choosing the Perfect Crockpot**

Selecting the right Crockpot is a critical step in your journey to becoming a master of slow cooking. With various sizes, features, and options on the market, it's essential to choose a Crockpot that aligns with your cooking preferences and requirements. Here are some factors to consider when selecting the perfect Crockpot:

1. Size Matters:

Crockpots come in a range of sizes, typically measured in quarts. The size you choose should depend on the number of people you typically cook for and the types of dishes you plan to prepare. for example, if you have limited space in your refrigerator, or need to cook for one or a maximum of two people, a three to four-quart Crockpot may suffice. If you often cook for a family or want to have leftovers, consider a six to seven-quart Crockpot. Larger models are available for large gatherings and special occasions.

2. Temperature Settings:

Most Crockpots offer two temperature settings: "high" and "low." Some may also have a "keep warm" setting. While these settings provide basic control over the cooking process, they are generally sufficient for most slow-cooked dishes. However, if you desire more precise temperature control, you may want to consider a model with additional heat settings, which some brands offer.

3. Programmable Timers:

The convenience of a programmable timer cannot be overstated. It allows you to set your Crockpot to start cooking at a specific time and automatically switch to the "keep warm" setting once the cooking time is complete. This feature is particularly useful if you're away from home during the day but want to return to a hot, ready-to-eat meal.

4. Material of the Pot:

Crockpot pots are typically made from either ceramic or stainless steel (inox). Ceramic pots tend to distribute heat more evenly, which can be advantageous for slow cooking. Stainless steel pots are known for their durability and easy cleaning. Consider your cooking preferences and whether even heat distribution or easy maintenance is more important to you.

5. Lid Design:

Crockpot lids are often made of glass with a tight-fitting seal. The transparent lid allows you to monitor your cooking without lifting it, which helps retain heat and moisture. Some lids have clips or latches, providing a secure seal for travel or transport, which can be useful if you plan to take your Crockpot to potlucks or gatherings.

6. Brand and Model:

There are various brands and models available, and while Crockpot is a well-known brand, other manufacturers produce high-quality slow cookers. Research the reputation, customer reviews, and features of different models to find one that suits your needs and budget.

7. Budget Considerations:

Crockpots are available at various price points. It's important to set a budget that aligns with your needs and preferences. While it's tempting to go for the top-of-the-line model, there are plenty of reliable and affordable options that can produce fantastic results.

8. Additional Features:

Some Crockpots come with additional features like hinged lids, temperature probes, and stovetop-safe pots for browning before slow cooking. Consider whether these extra features are essential for your cooking style.

In your journey to choose the perfect Crockpot, remember that it should align with your cooking needs and lifestyle. Whether you're looking for simplicity, advanced features, or the perfect size, the right Crockpot can make your slow-cooking experience a true pleasure. Take your time to explore your options, and you'll be rewarded with a kitchen companion that transforms ordinary ingredients into extraordinary meals.

1. Portion Control:

Cooking in a Crockpot often yields generous portions. While this is fantastic for sharing meals with family and friends, it can be a drawback if you're cooking for one or two. In this case, having a smaller Crockpot can help you maintain portion control and avoid excessive leftovers.

3. Cooking Time:

The size of your Crockpot also affects cooking times. Smaller Crockpots will heat up and cook faster than larger ones. If you have a smaller Crockpot but want to prepare a recipe designed for a larger model, you may need to adjust the cooking time accordingly. Conversely, if you have a larger Crockpot and want to cook a recipe designed for a smaller one, the cooking time might be quicker than expected.

4. Recipe Adaptation:

Consider the recipes you plan to prepare. Most slow cooker recipes specify the recommended Crockpot size. Adhering to these recommendations ensures that the dish cooks evenly and reaches the desired consistency. If you frequently adapt recipes to fit your Crockpot, make sure you adjust the ingredients and cooking times accordingly.

5. Storage and Convenience:

The size of your Crockpot can also affect storage. Smaller models are easier to store, especially if you have limited kitchen space. Larger Crockpots may require more storage room but offer the advantage of accommodating bigger cuts of meat or larger batches of ingredients.

6. Occasional Use:

If you plan to use your Crockpot for occasional gatherings or special occasions, a larger model might be practical. It can handle big portions and save you time when cooking for a crowd.

CHAPTER 3: CROCKPOT TOOLS AND ACCESSORIES

- **Equipping Your Kitchen for Crockpot Success**

TTo confidently begin your Crockpot culinary adventure, it's crucial to have your kitchen outfitted with the necessary equipment and accessories. Here's a rundown of the key essentials that will aid in your Crockpot cooking achievements:

1. Wooden Spatula or Spoon:

A wooden spatula or spoon is essential for stirring ingredients in your Crockpot. Unlike metal utensils, wooden ones won't scratch the non-stick surface of the pot.

2. Egg Steamer Rack

With this steamer rack, preparing hard-boiled eggs in the crockpot becomes a simple task, offering a great chance to familiarize yourself with the appliance. The eggs come out perfectly and are incredibly easy to peel. Utilizing a rack like this enables the simultaneous cooking of numerous eggs efficiently.

3. Food Thermometer:

A food thermometer is invaluable when cooking meat in your Crockpot. It allows you to check the internal temperature, ensuring that your meat is thoroughly cooked and safe to eat. Different meats have different safe temperature ranges, so having a reliable food thermometer is essential.

4. Slow Cooker Liners:

Slow cooker liners are optional but can be a time-saving convenience. They make cleanup a breeze by preventing food from sticking to the pot's surface. If you want to simplify the post-cooking cleanup process, consider using these liners.

5. Lid Holders:

Wave goodbye to cluttered and chaotic countertop spaces! This remarkable foldable gadget ensures your slow cooker's lid is held in the perfect spot, just above the pot's rim, for a tidy cooking area.

6. Springform Bundt Pan:

For baking desserts like cornbread, cheesecakes, lava cakes, and monkey bread using the "pot in pot" technique, this seven-inch diameter bundt pan is essential. Possessing such a pan opens up a plethora of recipe options for any baking endeavor.

7. Cooking Spray or Oil Mister:

A cooking spray or oil mister can help prevent sticking and make it easier to release the cooked food from your Crockpot. It's particularly useful for recipes that have a tendency to stick, like cheese-laden dishes.

8. Plastic Wrap or Foil Covers:

For recipes that require sealing the Crockpot with plastic wrap or foil, having these on hand is essential to ensure your dish cooks correctly and retains moisture.

9. Silicone Cooking Rack: it's recommended to invest in silicone trivets, pans, and tools to safeguard the crockpot's inner pot coating from damage.

10. Timer or Alarm Clock:

A timer or alarm clock is useful for tracking the cooking time of your Crockpot recipes. It ensures you don't overcook or undercook your dishes and that they're ready when you are.

11. Silicone Steam Basket:

This basket's included handles greatly simplify the lifting process. Its size is ample for holding fish fillets, and its tall sides ensure that water does not interfere with your cooking.

12. Trivets or Hot Pads:

Protect your countertops and dining table by using trivets or hot pads to place your hot Crockpot on. These prevent heat damage and ensure safe serving.

13. Colander:

A colander is useful for draining ingredients like pasta or beans before adding them to your Crockpot recipes.

14. Disposable Liners:

These convenient tools allow for swift and effortless cleanup after cooking a meal in a crockpot. They offer an excellent method to save time!

15. Mini Springform Pans:

These can function similarly to ramekins for crafting petite, single-serving meals. Given their size, they're perfectly suited for making homemade "egg muffins" as a breakfast option.

16. Airtight Storage Containers:

After you've cooked your delicious Crockpot meals, airtight storage containers help you safely store any leftovers and keep them fresh for longer.

With these essential Crockpot tools and equipment at your disposal, your kitchen will be fully equipped to tackle any slow-cooked recipe. These tools will make your Crockpot cooking experience efficient, enjoyable, and, most importantly, successful.

17. Silicone Oven Mitts:

This utensil proves invaluable for handling a warm crockpot in the kitchen, thanks to its textured, non-slip surface.

- **The Nice-to-Have Accessories**

While the essential tools and equipment are the foundation of your Crockpot kitchen, there are some additional accessories that can elevate your cooking experience and provide extra convenience. Consider adding these "nice-to-have" accessories to your kitchen collection:

1. Crockpot Travel Bag:

If you often transport your Crockpot for potlucks, gatherings, or family events, a dedicated Crockpot travel bag can be a game-changer. These insulated bags help keep your dish warm during transportation and protect your Crockpot from bumps and scratches.

2. Crockpot Lid Straps:

Lid straps are handy for securing the Crockpot lid during transportation, preventing spills and accidents. They're particularly useful when you're bringing your slow-cooked creations to gatherings.

3. Meat Shredding Claws:

These claw-like utensils are designed for shredding cooked meats like pulled pork or chicken effortlessly. They save time and make the process of pulling meat into tender, succulent strands a breeze.

4. Slow Cooker Recipe Books:

Investing in a good collection of slow cooker recipe books can provide you with a wealth of culinary inspiration and a variety of recipes to explore. It's an excellent resource to help you expand your Crockpot repertoire.

5. Digital Meat Thermometer:

While a basic food thermometer is essential, a digital meat thermometer with additional features like remote monitoring or wireless connectivity can be a convenient addition to your kitchen, allowing you to keep an eye on the internal temperature of your dishes without constantly checking.

6. Crockpot Food Warmer:

A Crockpot food warmer is a convenient accessory for keeping your slow-cooked dishes warm during parties and gatherings. It allows you to serve your creations buffet-style without the need for reheating.

7. Temperature Probe:

A temperature probe can be especially useful if you're cooking large cuts of meat or whole poultry in your Crockpot. It allows you to monitor the internal temperature of your dish with precision and ensure it's perfectly cooked.

8. Sous Vide Precision Cooker:

For the adventurous cook, a sous vide precision cooker can add an exciting dimension to your Crockpot cooking. It allows you to precisely control the temperature and achieve restaurant-quality results for certain dishes.

9. Digital Kitchen Scale:

A digital kitchen scale is a handy tool for accurate ingredient measurement, especially for recipes that require precise quantities.

10. Slow Cooker Bags:

These disposable, heat-resistant bags can simplify the cleanup process by preventing food from sticking to the Crockpot, similar to slow cooker liners. They are convenient for reducing post-cooking mess.

11. Crockpot Carrying Case:

For the frequent traveler with a Crockpot, a carrying case provides protection and convenience when transporting your slow cooker.

12. Silicone Slow Cooker Lid Holder:
A silicone lid holder is designed to keep your Crockpot lid upright and off the counter, helping maintain a clean and organized cooking space.

These "nice-to-have" accessories can enhance your Crockpot cooking experience by adding convenience and versatility to your kitchen. While they may not be essential for every cook, they can make your culinary adventures more enjoyable and efficient, allowing you to explore new recipes and cooking techniques with ease.

- **Handling Your Crockpot with Care**

Crockpot cooking is not only about creating delicious meals; it's also about ensuring safety and efficient operation. Here are some key guidelines for handling your Crockpot with care:

1. Read the User Manual:
Before using your Crockpot, familiarize yourself with the manufacturer's instructions provided in the user manual. This will help you understand the specific features and safety guidelines for your particular model.

2. Place Your Crockpot on a Stable Surface:
Ensure that your Crockpot is placed on a stable, flat surface to prevent accidental tipping or spilling. Avoid placing it near the edge of countertops or tables.

3. Handle the Crockpot with Oven Mitts or Towels:
The exterior of the Crockpot can become very hot during cooking. Always use oven mitts or towels when handling the unit to avoid burns.

4. Avoid Sudden Temperature Changes:
Do not expose the ceramic or inox pot to extreme temperature changes, such as transferring it directly from the refrigerator to the Crockpot or placing it on a cold surface immediately after cooking. Sudden temperature changes can lead to cracking.

5. Use Lid Holders:
When removing the lid, use the built-in lid holders (if available) or set it aside on a heat-resistant surface. Placing the hot lid directly on countertops can cause damage.

6. Check the Power Cord:
Inspect the power cord for any damage or fraying before use. A damaged cord can pose a safety risk and should be replaced.

7. Keep the Lid Sealed:
During cooking, avoid frequently lifting the lid to check on the progress of your dish. Each time you lift the lid, heat and moisture escape, potentially affecting the cooking time and the final result.

8. Follow Recipe Instructions:
Adhere to the cooking times and temperature settings specified in your recipes. Overcooking or undercooking can impact the taste and texture of your dishes.

9. Use Slow Cooker Liners for Easy Cleanup:
Consider using slow cooker liners or non-stick cooking spray to prevent food from sticking to the pot and make cleanup more straightforward.

10. Monitor the Liquid Levels:

Ensure there's enough liquid in your Crockpot to prevent your ingredients from drying out. However, be mindful not to overfill the pot, as it may result in spillovers during cooking.

11. Place Crockpot Away from Edges:

To reduce the risk of accidental contact, keep your Crockpot away from the edge of countertops, tables, or any surface where it could be bumped or knocked over.

12. Unplug When Not in Use:

After cooking, always unplug your Crockpot from the electrical outlet. Even if the Crockpot is turned off, leaving it plugged in poses no benefit and is a potential safety hazard.

13. Clean and Store Properly:

After use, clean your Crockpot according to the manufacturer's recommendations. Store it in a dry and safe location, avoiding exposure to moisture or extreme temperatures.

14. Inspect the Crockpot for Wear and Tear:

Regularly check your Crockpot for any signs of wear, damage, or malfunction. If you notice any issues, discontinue use and consult the manufacturer or a professional for repairs or replacement.

By handling your Crockpot with care and following these guidelines, you can ensure safe and efficient cooking experiences. Crockpot cooking is not only about creating delicious meals but also about creating them with peace of mind, knowing you're taking all necessary precautions for a successful and safe culinary journey.

- **Lid Materials: Inox or Ceramic?**

One of the decisions you may encounter when choosing a Crockpot is whether to opt for a lid made of stainless steel (Inox) or ceramic. Both materials have their advantages, and the choice largely depends on your preferences and cooking style.

1. Stainless Steel (Inox) Lids:

Pros:

- **Durability:** Inox lids are highly durable and resistant to damage. They can withstand wear and tear, making them a long-lasting choice.
- **Ease of Cleaning:** Stainless steel lids are relatively easy to clean. They are often dishwasher-safe and can handle regular washing without staining or discoloration.
- **Heat Retention:** Inox lids can help retain heat efficiently, keeping your slow-cooked dishes warm.

Cons:

- **Weight:** Stainless steel lids tend to be heavier, which may affect portability and handling when removing the lid during cooking.
- **Condensation:** Stainless steel lids may not trap condensation as effectively as ceramic lids, potentially leading to some moisture loss during the cooking process.

2. Ceramic Lids:

Pros:

- **Even Heat Distribution:** Ceramic lids often distribute heat more evenly, which can help maintain consistent cooking temperatures and reduce hot spots in your Crockpot.
- **Moisture Retention:** Ceramic lids can retain more moisture within the Crockpot, preventing the drying out of your dishes and enhancing the tenderness of meats and vegetables.
- **Aesthetic Appeal:** Ceramic lids may come in various decorative designs and colors, adding a touch of aesthetic appeal to your kitchen.

Cons:

- **Fragility:** Ceramic lids are more fragile than stainless steel lids and can be prone to chipping or breaking if mishandled or exposed to extreme temperature changes.
- **Maintenance:** While they are visually appealing, ceramic lids may require more careful handling and cleaning to prevent damage or staining.

In summary, your choice between Inox and ceramic lids for your Crockpot depends on your priorities. If you value durability and ease of cleaning, stainless steel (Inox) lids might be the better option. On the other hand, if even heat distribution and moisture retention are essential for your cooking style, ceramic lids can enhance the quality of your slow-cooked dishes.

Consider how you intend to use your Crockpot, the type of recipes you prefer, and your aesthetic preferences when making this decision. Whichever material you choose, proper care and maintenance will ensure that your Crockpot lid serves you well in your culinary adventures.

CHAPTER 4: TIPS AND TRICKS FOR CROCKPOT COOKING

- **Mastering the Art of Crockpot Cuisine**

To master the Art of Crockpot cooking consider the following tips and strategies:

1. Plan Your Meals:

Begin by planning your Crockpot meals. Think about the dishes you want to prepare, gather the necessary ingredients, and create a cooking schedule. This preparation will save you time and stress on busy days.

2. Know Your Crockpot:

Familiarize yourself with the features and settings of your Crockpot. Understand how to adjust cooking times and temperatures to match your recipes. Some models have additional functions like sautéing or browning, which can be valuable for certain recipes.

4. Brown Meat When Needed:

For recipes that benefit from a richer flavor and texture, consider browning meat before placing it in the Crockpot. This step adds depth to stews, roasts, and other savory dishes.

5. Use Fresh Ingredients:

Whenever possible, use fresh ingredients to enhance the flavor of your dishes. Fresh herbs, spices, and produce can make a substantial difference in the final taste of your slow-cooked meals.

6. Properly Measure Ingredients:

Accurate measurements are essential for successful cooking. Use measuring cupful and spoons to ensure you're adding the right quantities of liquid, spices, and seasonings.

7. Adapt Recipes to Your Crockpot:

Crockpots come in various sizes, so it's essential to adjust recipes to match the capacity of your specific model. Recipes designed for larger Crockpots may require modification for smaller units and vice versa.

8. Mind the Liquid Levels:

Be mindful of the liquid levels in your Crockpot. Too much liquid can result in a watery dish, while too little can lead to dryness. Follow recipe guidelines or adjust as needed.

9. Add Delicate Ingredients Later:

Some ingredients, like dairy products, seafood, or tender vegetables, can become overcooked if added too early. Incorporate these ingredients later in the cooking process to preserve their integrity.

10. Practice Patience:

One of the key principles of Crockpot cooking is patience. Resist the temptation to lift the lid frequently; each time you do, heat and moisture escape, potentially affecting the cooking time and results.

11. Experiment and Learn:

Crockpot cooking is a journey of experimentation and discovery. Try new recipes, explore diverse cuisines, and learn from both successes and failures. You'll gradually develop an intuition for crafting exceptional slow-cooked dishes.

12. Enjoy the Aromas:

Crockpot cooking fills your home with tantalizing aromas. Savor the anticipation as your meal gradually takes shape, and relish the delicious scents that waft through your kitchen.

13. Share Your Creations:

Part of mastering Crockpot cuisine is sharing your delicious creations with family and friends. Host potluck dinners, invite loved ones to savor your dishes, and enjoy the communal aspect of slow cooking.

14. Keep a Crockpot Journal:

Maintain a Crockpot journal where you record your recipes, modifications, and cooking times. This reference can help you refine your skills and replicate successful dishes.

15. Embrace Creativity:

Don't be afraid to get creative with your Crockpot. Modify existing recipes, create your own, and personalize dishes to suit your tastes. Crockpot cuisine is a canvas for culinary expression.

With patience, practice, and a willingness to experiment, you can truly master the art of Crockpot cuisine. As you hone your skills and develop a deep understanding of your Crockpot's capabilities, you'll be able to create an array of delicious, slow-cooked masterpieces that will delight your taste buds and those of your loved ones.

- **Layering Food Like a Pro**

Layering ingredients in your Crockpot is a fundamental skill that can greatly influence the outcome of your slow-cooked dishes. Proper layering ensures even cooking and allows flavors to meld harmoniously. Here's how to layer food like a pro:

1. Start with a Clean Crockpot:

Before layering, make sure your Crockpot is clean and dry. A clean surface prevents food from sticking and ensures easy cleanup.

2. Begin with the Right Base:

Start with the main ingredient that requires the longest cooking time. This is typically the meat or protein. Place it at the bottom of the Crockpot to ensure it cooks thoroughly.

3. Add Hard Vegetables Next:

If your recipe includes hard vegetables like carrots, potatoes, or root vegetables, place them on top of the meat. These vegetables take longer to cook, and placing them closer to the heat source ensures they become tender.

4. Incorporate Grains or Pasta Sparingly:

If your recipe involves grains or pasta, add them as a separate layer, but use them sparingly. Place them on top of the vegetables to prevent them from overcooking and becoming mushy. It's also a good idea to slightly undercook grains and pasta before adding them to the Crockpot.

5. Distribute Aromatics and Seasonings:

Layer aromatic ingredients like garlic, onions, and spices on top of the vegetables. This allows their flavors to infuse the entire dish. Distribute them evenly for a balanced taste.

6. Liquid Is Essential:

Pour the liquid component of your recipe over the layered ingredients. This ensures even distribution of flavors and helps maintain the right level of moisture during cooking. It's important not to overfill with liquid, as it can lead to a soupy outcome.

7. Dairy and Cheese:

Dairy products like cream, milk, or cheese should be introduced towards the end of the cooking process. Adding them too early can result in curdling or separation. Stir in dairy or cheese shortly before serving, and allow them to melt and blend with the other ingredients.

8. Delicate Ingredients at the Top:

If your recipe includes more delicate ingredients like leafy greens, fresh herbs, or seafood, add them in the final layer. These ingredients require less cooking time and should be placed closer to the surface.

9. Use Foil or Parchment Dividers:

For recipes that involve ingredients that shouldn't mix, use foil or parchment paper dividers. This prevents flavors from intermingling while still allowing them to cook simultaneously.

10. Minimize Stirring:

Resist the temptation to stir your Crockpot ingredients frequently. Frequent stirring can lead to heat loss and interfere with the layers' cooking process. Trust the slow cooking method to blend flavors naturally.

11. Maintain Even Distribution:

As you layer, aim for even distribution of ingredients. This helps ensure that every serving contains a balanced mix of flavors and textures.

12. Monitor Cooking Times:

Be mindful of the recommended cooking times for each layer. If your recipe specifies different cooking times for various ingredients, stagger their addition to the Crockpot accordingly.

13. Garnish at the End:

Fresh herbs, cheese, or garnishes should be added just before serving. These final touches enhance the appearance and flavor of your dish.

By mastering the art of layering, you'll create Crockpot dishes that are not only delicious but also visually appealing. Your ingredients will cook to perfection, resulting in a harmonious and satisfying culinary experience. Layering food like a pro is the secret to slow-cooked success.

- **Seasoning and Spicing Up Your Dishes**

The art of Crockpot cooking extends beyond just choosing ingredients and layering them. It involves adding the right seasonings and spices to create a symphony of flavors. Here's how to season and spice up your dishes effectively:

1. Start with the Basics:

Begin with fundamental seasonings like salt and pepper. These are the building blocks of flavor and enhance the taste of all other ingredients. Season your protein (meat, poultry, or seafood) generously with salt and pepper before placing it in the Crockpot.

2. Layer Aromatics:

Aromatics such as onions, garlic, and ginger are your flavor foundation. Distribute these evenly among your layers, ensuring they infuse the entire dish with their aromatic essence. Sautéing them briefly before adding to the Crockpot can intensify their flavors.

3. Utilize Fresh Herbs:

Fresh herbs like rosemary, thyme, basil, and parsley bring vibrancy to your slow-cooked dishes. Add them as the final layer, placing them on top to preserve their delicate flavors. Alternatively, you can garnish your plated servings with fresh herbs for an aromatic finish.

4. Experiment with Spices:

Spices are the key to adding complexity to your Crockpot creations. Explore a range of spices, such as cumin, paprika, coriander, cinnamon, and chili powder. Spice blends like curry powder or garam masala can lend unique character to your dishes. Be mindful of the quantity; a little goes a long way, and spices may intensify as the dish cooks.

5. Think About Seasoned Broths:

For added depth, consider using seasoned broths or stocks. These liquid seasonings can infuse your dish with complex flavors. Options include chicken, beef, vegetable, or seafood broth, as well as bouillon cubes or powdered stock.

6. Sweet and Savory Balancing:

Balancing sweet and savory flavors can be magical. Ingredients like brown sugar, honey, maple syrup, or molasses can impart a touch of sweetness to counterbalance savory and spicy elements. Experiment with these sweet accents in dishes like pulled pork or chili.

7. Acidic Notes:

Don't forget about acidic elements like citrus juice, vinegar, or tomatoes. A splash of lemon juice or a drizzle of balsamic vinegar can brighten and balance the overall taste of your dishes.

8. Wine and Spirits:

Incorporate wine, beer, or spirits for a sophisticated layer of flavor. These liquids can deglaze pans, intensify tastes, and bring complexity to dishes. Red wine, for instance, works well in beef stew, while white wine pairs beautifully with chicken or seafood.

9. Taste and Adjust:

Taste your Crockpot creation as it cooks and adjust the seasonings as needed. Keep in mind that flavors may concentrate during the slow-cooking process, so a subtle hand is key. You can add more salt, herbs, or spices to achieve the desired taste.

10. Finish with Freshness:

To brighten up your dishes, consider adding fresh ingredients like lemon zest, grated Parmesan cheese, or chopped scallions just before serving. These finishing touches add a burst of flavor and freshness.

11. Keep a Flavor Journal:
Maintain a flavor journal where you record your seasoning experiments, including what worked well and what didn't. This reference will help you refine your seasoning skills and create unforgettable dishes.

Seasoning and spicing up your Crockpot dishes is an opportunity to express your culinary creativity. By mastering the art of balancing and enhancing flavors, you'll transform ordinary ingredients into extraordinary meals. Experiment, trust your taste buds, and savor the delightful results of your seasoned and spiced Crockpot creations.

CHAPTER 5: CLEANING, MAINTENANCE, AND RESOURCES

- **The Aftermath: Cleaning Your Crockpot**

After relishing a delightful meal prepared in your slow cooker, you must tackle the necessary chore of cleaning your Crockpot. Thorough cleaning is crucial not just for extending the life of your appliance, but also for prepping it for your upcoming cooking exploits. Below is a detailed, step-by-step guide to efficiently clean your Crockpot:

1. Unplug and Cool Down:

Before you start cleaning, unplug your Crockpot and allow it to cool down. Attempting to clean it while hot can result in burns or damage.

2. Remove the Insert:

Take out the ceramic or Inox insert from the base of the Crockpot. These inserts are typically removable and dishwasher-safe. If your model allows, detach any other removable components.

3. Dispose of Excess Food:

Dispose of any remaining food or liquids in the insert. Scrape off any stubborn bits with a non-abrasive utensil, like a wooden or plastic spatula.

4. Soak the Insert:

Fill the Crockpot insert with warm, soapy water and allow it to soak for a while. This will help loosen any stuck-on food residue.

5. Hand Wash or Use a Dishwasher:

After soaking, gently scrub the insert with a non-abrasive sponge or cloth. Avoid abrasive scouring pads or steel wool, as they can damage the surface. If your Crockpot insert is dishwasher-safe, you can run it through a dishwasher cycle. However, hand washing is generally recommended for prolonged durability.

6. Clean the Base:

Wipe down the base of the Crockpot with a damp cloth to remove any spills or splatters. Be cautious not to let water seep into the electrical components, and never immerse the base in water.

7. Lid and Lid Sealing Gasket:

Clean the lid, including the sealing gasket, with warm, soapy water. Some lids are dishwasher-safe, but check the manufacturer's instructions. Be sure to remove the gasket and clean it separately if it's detachable.

8. Dealing with Stains or Residue:

If you encounter stubborn stains or residue, mix a paste of baking soda and water. Apply this paste to the affected areas and let it sit for a while before gently scrubbing.

9. Rinse Thoroughly:

After cleaning, rinse all components thoroughly with clean water to remove any soap residue.

10. Dry Completely:

Allow all parts of the Crockpot to air-dry completely. Ensure there is no trapped moisture before reassembling or storing.

11. Reassemble and Store:

Once dry, reassemble your Crockpot, placing the insert back onto the base. Store it in a dry, cool place, ensuring it's free from moisture to prevent odors or damage.

12. Regular Maintenance:

Clean your Crockpot after each use to prevent the buildup of stubborn residue. This will make future cleanings easier and ensure your Crockpot remains in pristine condition.

13. Deep Cleaning:

Periodically, perform a deep cleaning by removing any mineral deposits or discoloration from the insert using a mixture of equal parts water and white vinegar. Allow the mixture to sit in the insert for several hours or overnight, then scrub and rinse thoroughly.

By following these cleaning steps, you'll maintain your Crockpot in excellent condition and be ready for your next culinary adventure. Regular maintenance and proper cleaning ensure your Crockpot continues to serve you in creating delicious, slow-cooked meals for years to come.

- **Tips to Prevent Scratching the Bottom**

Scratching the bottom of your Crockpot's ceramic or Inox insert can diminish its effectiveness and lifespan. To keep your Crockpot in pristine condition, consider these helpful tips to prevent scratching the bottom:

Use Proper Utensils:

- When cooking in your Crockpot, use utensils that won't scratch the surface of the insert, such as wooden, plastic or silicon utensils. Avoid metal utensils that can damage the ceramic or Inox coating.

By following these maintenance tips, you can ensure that your Crockpot remains in excellent condition, providing you with countless delicious, slow-cooked meals. With proper care and attention, your Crockpot will continue to be a reliable and cherished addition to your kitchen for years to come.

1. Gentle Stirring:

When stirring or adjusting the contents of your Crockpot, do so gently. Avoid vigorous stirring or scraping the bottom with force, as this can lead to scratches over time.

2. Pre-soak Stuck-on Food:

If food becomes stuck to the bottom during cooking, resist the urge to scrape it off forcefully. Instead, soak the insert in warm, soapy water after removing the meal. This will help loosen the stuck-on food, making it easier to clean without damaging the surface.

3. Deglaze Carefully:

When deglazing the bottom of the insert to release flavorful bits, use a wooden or plastic spatula. Avoid using metal utensils for this purpose to prevent scratching the surface.

4. Line with Crockpot Liners:

Consider using Crockpot liners, which are disposable plastic bags designed to fit your Crockpot's insert. These liners prevent food from coming into direct contact with the insert, reducing the risk of scratching.

5. Layer Ingredients Strategically:

Properly layering ingredients can help prevent scraping. Start with your protein or meat at the bottom and avoid placing it directly on the hot surface. Use a layer of vegetables or other ingredients between the protein and the surface to protect it.

6. Season the Bottom:

Lightly season the bottom of the insert with oil or non-stick cooking spray before adding ingredients. This can create a protective layer that minimizes the risk of sticking and scratching.

7. Properly Store Utensils:

Store your Crockpot utensils separately from other kitchen tools. Make sure they are in a location where they won't accidentally come into contact with sharp or metal utensils that can potentially cause scratches.

By following these tips, you can maintain the bottom of your Crockpot's insert in excellent condition, ensuring that it continues to serve you well in creating delicious, slow-cooked meals without the risk of damage or unsightly scratches.

- **Handy Conversion Tables**

Cooking is an art that often requires precision, especially when following recipes. To assist you in your culinary journey, here are handy conversion tables to help you easily translate measurements and temperatures between various systems:

1. Measurement Conversions:

Use this table to convert common cooking measurements between the American System and the European System. Having this reference at hand can be immensely helpful when working with recipes from different regions.

Measurement	American System	European System
one teaspoonful (tsp)	five milliliters	five milliliters
one tablespoonful (tbsp)	fifteen milliliters	fifteen milliliters
one fluid ounce (fl oz)	30 milliliters	2eight milliliters

Measurement	American System	European System
one cupful	240 milliliters	250 milliliters
one pint (pt)	480 milliliters	500 milliliters
one quart (qt)	0.9five liters	one liter
one gallon (gal)	3.eight liters	four liters
one ounce (oz)	2eight grams	30 grams
one pound (lb)	45four grams	500 grams

2. Temperature Conversions:

This table provides temperature conversions between Fahrenheit and Celsius, allowing you to easily switch between these two common temperature scales when cooking or baking.

Temperature (°F)	Temperature (°C)
-40°F	-40°C
-4°F	-20°C
32°F	0°C
212°F	100°C
250°F	121°C
300°F	149°C
350°F	177°C
400°F	204°C
450°F	232°C
500°F	260°C

3. Oven Temperature Conversion:

For those who frequently work with recipes that specify temperatures in gas marks, this table helps you convert gas marks to Fahrenheit and Celsius for accurate oven settings.

Gas Mark	Fahrenheit	Celsius
1	275°F	140°C
2	300°F	150°C
3	325°F	165°C
4	350°F	180°C
5	375°F	190°C
6	400°F	200°C
7	425°F	220°C
8	450°F	230°C
9	475°F	240°C

These conversion tables will prove invaluable in your Crockpot cooking adventures, making it easier to follow recipes from around the world and maintain the precision required for successful dishes. Whether you need to convert measurements, temperatures, or gas marks, these tables will be your reliable reference.

- **Valuable Industry References and Links**

In the world of Crockpot cooking, there are numerous industry references, websites, and books that offer valuable insights, recipes, and tips. These resources can enhance your Crockpot culinary journey and keep you updated on the latest trends and techniques. Here are some notable industry references and links to explore:

1. Crock-Pot® Official Website
- Website: Crock-Pot®

2. America's Test Kitchen - Slow Cooker from America's Test Kitchen
- Website: America's Test Kitchen

3. The Kitchn - Slow Cooker Section
- Website: The Kitchn

4. AllRecipes - Slow Cooker Recipes
- Website: AllRecipes

5. Reddit's Slow Cooking Community
- Reddit Community: r/slowcooking

6. The Crockin' Girls

- Website: <u>The Crockin' Girls</u>
7. Cooking Light - Slow Cooker Recipes
- Website: <u>Cooking Light</u>
8. Eat Well 10one - Slow Cooker Recipes
- Website: <u>Eat Well 101</u>
9. "Crockpot 365" Blog by Stephanie O'Dea
- Blog: <u>Crockpot 365</u>
10. Pinterest - Crockpot Recipes
- Website: <u>Pinterest</u>

These industry references, websites, and books offer a wide range of resources for Crockpot cooking, from official manufacturers to reputable cooking communities and influential authors. They provide valuable knowledge, recipes, and community interaction to support and enrich your Crockpot culinary experience. Explore these resources to expand your culinary horizons and elevate your Crockpot cooking skills.

OVEN TO CROCK POT CONVERSION TABLE

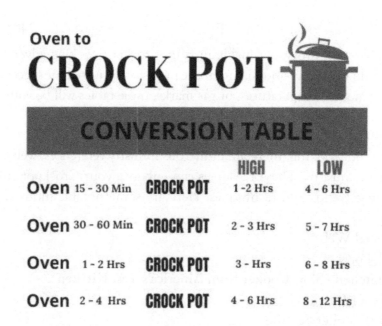

CHAPTER 6: FREQUENTLY ASKED QUESTIONS (FAQ)

- **Common Crockpot Cooking Questions**

Crockpot cooking, while wonderfully convenient, can sometimes raise questions and uncertainties. Here are answers to some of the most common inquiries that arise during your Crockpot culinary journey:

1. Can I Use Frozen Ingredients?

- It's generally recommended to use thawed ingredients for even cooking. Starting with frozen ingredients can slow down the cooking process and might result in unevenly cooked dishes.

2. Do I Need to Brown Meat Before Adding It to the Crockpot?

- While it's not mandatory, browning meat before adding it can enhance the flavor and texture of your dishes. Searing the meat in a hot pan before slow-cooking adds depth to the final results.

3. How Full Should I Fill the Crockpot?

- Crockpots should ideally be filled halfway to three-quarters full. Overfilling can lead to uneven cooking, while underfilling may result in food drying out. Follow your recipe's guidelines for the best results.

4. Can I put my crock pot in the microwave?

- The removable ceramic inserts of all crock pots can be safely microwaved and used in an oven up to 400°F, provided the lid is not attached. If you have a different brand of slow cooker, consult your user manual for guidance on the microwave and oven safety of the crockery insert.

5. Should I Stir the Ingredients While Cooking?

- Avoid frequent stirring, as Crockpots are designed for slow, steady cooking. Opening the lid and stirring too often can lead to heat loss and increased cooking time.

6. Can I Convert Oven or Stovetop Recipes to Crockpot Recipes?

- Yes, many oven and stovetop recipes can be adapted for the Crockpot. However, adjustments in cooking times and liquid amounts may be needed. Consult Crockpot-specific recipes or cooking guides for guidance.

Troubleshooting Crockpot Issues

Crockpots are generally reliable, but occasional issues can arise. Here's a troubleshooting guide to address common Crockpot problems:

1. Food Is Overcooked and Dry:

- If your food turns out overcooked and dry, reduce the cooking time in your next recipe. You can also try adding more liquid to maintain moisture.

2. Food Is Undercooked:

- If you find that your food is undercooked, ensure your Crockpot is set to the correct temperature setting. Additionally, check the freshness of your ingredients.

3. Slow Cooking Takes Too Long:

- If your Crockpot takes longer than expected, ensure that it's plugged in correctly and the power source is working. Also, avoid frequently lifting the lid, which can extend the cooking time.

4. Uneven Cooking:

- To address uneven cooking, ensure you're layering your ingredients properly, with harder items at the bottom and softer items on top. Stirring sparingly and adding enough liquid can help too.

5. Stuck-On Food Residue:

- If you're having trouble cleaning the insert due to stuck-on food residue, try soaking it in warm, soapy water before cleaning. For stubborn residue, use a mixture of baking soda and water to gently scrub.

6. Lid Doesn't Fit Properly:

- If the lid doesn't fit snugly, it can affect the cooking process. Check for any damage to the lid or the Crockpot's rim. If you find any issues, contact the manufacturer for a replacement.

By addressing common questions and troubleshooting issues, you can confidently navigate the world of Crockpot cooking, ensuring delicious results with each dish. Crockpot cooking can be a joyful and fulfilling experience, and with a little know-how, you'll be on your way to mastering this culinary art.

- **Expert Insights and Answers**

Embarking on a Crockpot culinary adventure can be a rewarding experience, but it's natural to have questions and seek expert insights to enhance your skills. Here are answers to some common questions and valuable insights from experts in the field of Crockpot cooking:

1. Q: How do I choose the right Crockpot for my needs?

Expert Advice: The right Crockpot depends on your specific requirements. Consider factors such as size, programmable features, and whether you prefer a digital or manual model. Think about the types of meals you want to prepare and choose a Crockpot that suits your lifestyle and cooking style.

2. Q: Can I use my Crockpot for more than just stews and soups?

Expert Advice: Absolutely! Crockpots are versatile and can be used for various dishes, including roasts, desserts, and even dips. Experiment with different recipes to explore the full range of possibilities.

3. Q: Can I leave my Crockpot unattended while cooking?

Expert Advice: Crockpots are designed to be left unattended while cooking, making them a convenient option for busy individuals. However, it's essential to follow recommended cooking times and settings to ensure safety and desired results. Always use your Crockpot within manufacturer guidelines.

4. Q: What's the secret to layering ingredients in a Crockpot for even cooking?

Expert Advice: To achieve even cooking, start by placing denser or harder ingredients at the bottom and softer items on top. This allows heat to circulate more effectively. Additionally, ensure there's adequate liquid to create a moist cooking environment.

5. Q: How do I adapt oven or stovetop recipes for the Crockpot?

Expert Advice: Adapting recipes for the Crockpot may require some adjustments. Reduce the liquid content by about one-third, as slow cooking retains more moisture. Adjust cooking times; dishes may cook faster or slower than conventional methods. Monitor the first time you try a conversion and make notes for future reference.

6. Q: Can I use my Crockpot for meal prepping or batch cooking?

Expert Advice: Crockpots are excellent tools for meal prepping and batch cooking. You can prepare large quantities of food and store it in portions for easy access to homemade, ready-made meals throughout the week. Just be sure to follow proper storage and reheating guidelines.

7. Q: Are there any specific safety tips for using a Crockpot?

Expert Advice: Safety is crucial. Always follow the manufacturer's instructions and never immerse the base in water. Ensure the Crockpot is placed on a stable, heat-resistant surface. Don't use a damaged or cracked insert, and unplug the Crockpot when not in use. For extended cooking times, consider using a timer.

These expert insights and answers can help you navigate the world of Crockpot cooking with confidence. Learning from seasoned Crockpot enthusiasts and professionals can enhance your skills and lead to delicious, stress-free cooking experiences.

- **Final Tips and Encouragement**

As you dive into the world of Crockpot cooking, we want to leave you with some final tips and a hearty dose of encouragement to ensure your culinary adventures are a resounding success:

1. Embrace Experimentation: Don't be afraid to get creative in your Crockpot endeavors. Try new ingredients, seasonings, and flavor combinations. Some of the most delicious dishes are born from a spirit of experimentation.

2. Patience Is a Virtue: Slow cooking is aptly named, and patience is key. The magic of the Crockpot unfolds gradually. Allow your dishes the time they need to develop rich flavors and tender textures.

3. Layer with Love: Properly layering your ingredients is vital for even cooking. Start with denser items at the bottom and softer items on top. This technique ensures that everything cooks to perfection.

4. Invest in Quality Ingredients: The quality of your ingredients greatly impacts the final taste of your dishes. Opt for fresh produce and high-quality meats for the best results.

5. Master Timing: Understand that not all ingredients should go into your Crockpot at the same time. Some require more cooking time, while others should be added later to preserve their texture and flavor. Timing is everything.

6. Prep Ahead: Save time and stress by prepping your ingredients the night before or in the morning. This way, you can simply toss everything into the Crockpot when it's time to cook.

7. Don't Fear Mistakes: Mistakes are part of any culinary journey. If a dish doesn't turn out as expected, don't be discouraged. Learn from the experience and use it to improve your skills.

8. Stay Curious: Keep your curiosity alive. There are countless Crockpot recipes and techniques to explore. Be open to learning and trying new things.

9. Share the Joy: Crockpot cooking can be a wonderful way to connect with loved ones. Share your delicious creations with family and friends, and revel in the joy of shared meals.

10. Embrace the Crockpot Lifestyle: Make Crockpot cooking a lifestyle, not just a cooking method. The convenience and versatility of the Crockpot can simplify meal preparation and enhance your culinary journey.

11. Seek Inspiration: Whether it's from cookbooks, online resources, or fellow Crockpot enthusiasts, seek inspiration to keep your cooking fresh and exciting.

12. Most Importantly, Enjoy the Journey: The joy of Crockpot cooking is not only in savoring the delicious dishes but also in the journey itself. Relish the process, from the aroma that fills your home to the satisfaction of sharing your creations with others.

We encourage you to dive into your Crockpot cooking adventure with enthusiasm and an open heart. With each dish you create, you'll build confidence and culinary prowess. Remember, the most important ingredient is your love for cooking, and that's something that can't be measured but will always shine through in your dishes. Happy Crockpot cooking!

CHAPTER 7: BREAKFAST

1. CROCKPOT BREAKFAST CASSEROLE

Servings: 2-3
Ingredients:
- Twelve large eggs
- one cupful milk
- one pound ground breakfast sausage, browned and drained
- two cupful shredded cheddar cheese
- one red bell pepper, diced
- one green bell pepper, diced
- one onion, diced
- one teaspoonful salt
- half teaspoonful black pepper
- Cooking spray

Instructions:
1. In a large bowl, whisk together eggs and milk. Season with salt and pepper.
2. Spray the inside of your Crockpot with cooking spray.
3. Layer the browned sausage, diced peppers, onions, and shredded cheese in the Crockpot.
4. Pour the egg mixture over the top.
5. Cook on low for six-eight hours or until eggs are set.
6. Serve and enjoy!

Duration for this recipe: six-eight hours on low
Nutrients (per portion): Caloric content: 320
- Amino content: 20g
- Carb content: 5g
- Fatty acid: 25g

2. CROCKPOT OATMEAL

Servings: 2-3
Ingredients:
- two cupful rolled oats
- four cupful water

- one cupful milk
- one-fourth cupful brown sugar
- one teaspoonful cinnamon
- half teaspoonful salt
- one cupful diced apples
- half cupful raisins
- one-fourth cupful chopped nuts (optional)

Instructions:

1. Combine rolled oats, water, milk, brown sugar, cinnamon, and salt in the Crockpot.

2. Stir in diced apples and raisins.

3. Cook on low for seven-eight hours or on high for three-four hours.

4. Serve with chopped nuts and additional brown sugar if desired.

Duration for this recipe: seven-eight hours on low, or three-four hours on high.

Nutrients (per portion):
- Caloric content: 260
- Amino content: 6g
- Carb content: 47g
- Fatty acid: 6g

3. CROCKPOT BREAKFAST BURRITO FILLING

Servings: 2-3

Ingredients:
- one pound ground breakfast sausage
- one small onion, diced
- one bell pepper, diced
- eight large eggs
- one-fourth cupful milk
- Salt and pepper to taste
- one cupful shredded cheddar cheese
- Flour tortillas

Instructions:

1. In a skillet, brown the sausage and drain excess fat.

2. In the same skillet, add diced onion and bell pepper. Sauté until softened.

3. In a bowl, whisk together eggs, milk, salt, and pepper.

4. Transfer the cooked sausage, onion, and bell pepper to the Crockpot. Pour the egg mixture over it.

5. Cook on low for three-four hours or until the eggs are set.

6. Serve the filling in flour tortillas and sprinkle with shredded cheddar cheese.

Duration for this recipe: three-four hours on low

Nutrients (per portion, not including tortilla):
- Caloric content: 280
- Amino content: 17g
- Carb content: 4g
- Fatty acid: 21g

4. CROCKPOT FRENCH TOAST CASSEROLE

Servings: 2-3

Ingredients:
- one loaf of French bread, cut into cubes
- eight large eggs
- two cupful milk
- half cupful heavy cream
- one-fourth cupful granulated sugar
- one-fourth cupful brown sugar
- two teaspoonful vanilla extract
- one teaspoonful ground cinnamon
- one-fourth teaspoonful ground nutmeg
- half cupful chopped pecans (optional)
- Maple syrup for serving

Instructions:

1. Grease the inside of your Crockpot.

2. Place the bread cubes in the Crockpot.

3. In a large bowl, whisk together the eggs, milk, heavy cream, granulated sugar, brown sugar, vanilla extract, cinnamon, and nutmeg.

4. Pour the egg mixture over the bread cubes.

5. Sprinkle chopped pecans on top.

6. Cook on low for four-six hours or until the center is set and the edges are golden.

7. Serve with maple syrup.

Duration for this recipe: four-six hours on low

Nutrients (per portion):
- Caloric content: 380

- Amino content: 14g
- Carb content: 37g
- Fatty acid: 21g

5. CROCKPOT BREAKFAST TACOS

Servings: 2-3
Ingredients:
- one pound ground breakfast sausage
- one small onion, diced
- one bell pepper, diced
- eight large eggs
- one-fourth cupful milk
- Salt and pepper to taste
- one cupful shredded cheddar cheese
- Flour tortillas
- Salsa and sour cream for serving

Instructions:
1. In a skillet, brown the sausage and drain excess fat.
2. In the same skillet, add diced onion and bell pepper. Sauté until softened.
3. In a bowl, whisk together eggs, milk, salt, and pepper.
4. Transfer the cooked sausage, onion, and bell pepper to the Crockpot. Pour the egg mixture over it.
5. Cook on low for three-four hours or until the eggs are set.
6. Serve the filling in flour tortillas, topped with shredded cheddar cheese, salsa, and sour cream.

Duration for this recipe: three-four hours on low

Nutrients (per portion, not including tortilla and toppings):
- Caloric content: 270
- Amino content: 17g
- Carb content: 3g
- Fatty acid: 20g

6. CROCKPOT BREAKFAST QUINOA

Servings: 4-6
Duration for this recipe: four-six hours on low
Ingredients:
- one cupful quinoa, rinsed

- two cupful milk
- one-fourth cupful honey
- half teaspoonful vanilla extract
- half teaspoonful ground cinnamon
- one-fourth teaspoonful ground nutmeg
- one-fourth cupful dried cranberries
- one-fourth cupful chopped almonds
- Fresh berries for topping

Instructions:
1. Combine quinoa, milk, honey, vanilla extract, cinnamon, and nutmeg in the Crockpot.
2. Stir in dried cranberries and chopped almonds.
3. Cook on low for four-six hours or until quinoa is tender and the mixture thickens.
4. Serve with fresh berries on top.

Nutrients (per portion):
- Caloric content: 330
- Amino content: 9g
- Carb content: 57g
- Fatty acid: 8g

7. CROCKPOT BREAKFAST BAKED BEANS

Servings: 2-3
Ingredients:
- two cans (fifteen oz each) of baked beans
- half cupful ketchup
- one-fourth cupful brown sugar
- one-fourth cupful diced onion
- one-fourth cupful diced bell pepper
- one-fourth cupful cooked and crumbled bacon
- one-fourth cupful maple syrup
- half teaspoonful ground mustard
- half teaspoonful garlic powder
- half teaspoonful black pepper

Instructions:
1. Combine all ingredients in the Crockpot and stir well.
2. Cook on low for three-four hours, stirring occasionally.
3. Serve as a hearty breakfast side dish.

Duration for this recipe: three-four hours on low

Nutrients (per portion):

- Caloric content: 240
- Amino content: 5g
- Carb content: 48g
- Fatty acid: 4g

8. CROCKPOT BLUEBERRY BREAKFAST CAKE

Duration for this recipe: two-three hours on low

Servings: 4-6

Ingredients:

- two cupful all-purpose flour
- half cupful granulated sugar
- half cupful brown sugar
- two teaspoonful baking powder
- half teaspoonful baking soda
- half teaspoonful salt
- two large eggs
- one cupful plain Greek yogurt
- one-fourth cupful unsalted butter, melted
- one teaspoonful vanilla extract
- one cupful fresh blueberries
- Cooking spray

Instructions:

1. In a large bowl, whisk together flour, granulated sugar, brown sugar, baking powder, baking soda, and salt.

2. In another bowl, beat the eggs and then add Greek yogurt, melted butter, and vanilla extract.

3. Combine the wet and dry ingredients.

4. Gently fold in the fresh blueberries.

5. Spray the inside of your Crockpot with cooking spray.

6. Pour the batter into the Crockpot.

7. Cook on low for two-three hours or until a toothpick comes out clean from the center.

8. Let the cake cool before serving.

Nutrients (per portion): Caloric content: 260, Amino content: 6g, Carb content: 45g, Fatty acid: 6g

9. CROCKPOT BREAKFAST FRITTATA

Servings: 2-3

Ingredients:

- ten large eggs
- half cupful milk
- one cupful diced ham
- half cupful diced bell pepper
- half cupful diced onion
- one cupful shredded cheddar cheese
- half teaspoonful salt
- one-fourth teaspoonful black pepper
- Cooking spray

Instructions:

1. In a large bowl, whisk together eggs and milk. Season with salt and pepper.

2. Spray the inside of your Crockpot with cooking spray.

3. Layer diced ham, bell pepper, onion, and shredded cheddar cheese in the Crockpot.

4. Pour the egg mixture over the top.

5. Cook on low for three-four hours or until eggs are set.

6. Serve and enjoy!

Duration for this recipe: three-four hours on low

Nutrients (per portion): Caloric content: 280, Amino content: 19g, Carb content: 4g, Fatty acid: 20g

10. CROCKPOT BREAKFAST QUICHE

Servings: 2-3

Ingredients:

- one frozen pie crust
- six large eggs
- one cupful milk
- one cupful diced ham
- half cupful shredded cheddar cheese
- half cupful diced bell pepper
- one-fourth cupful diced onion
- one-fourth cupful sliced mushrooms
- half teaspoonful salt
- one-fourth teaspoonful black pepper

Instructions:

1. Place the frozen pie crust in the Crockpot.

2.   In a bowl, whisk together eggs and milk. Season with salt and pepper.

3.   Layer diced ham, shredded cheddar cheese, bell pepper, onion, and mushrooms in the pie crust.

4.   Pour the egg mixture over the top.

5.   Cook on low for three-four hours or until the quiche is set and lightly browned.

6.   Allow it to cool slightly before slicing and serving.

Duration for this recipe: three-four hours on low

Nutrients (per portion): Caloric content: 320, Amino content: 16g, Carb content: 19g, Fatty acid: 20g

CHAPTER 8: BEANS AND GRAIN

1. CROCKPOT VEGETARIAN CHILI

Servings: 2-3

Ingredients:

- one cupful dried kidney beans, soaked and drained
- one cupful dried black beans, soaked and drained
- one cupful dried pinto beans, soaked and drained
- one onion, diced
- one bell pepper, diced
- three cloves garlic, minced
- 2eight oz canned diced tomatoes
- one cupful corn kernels
- two tablespoonful chili powder
- one teaspoonful cumin
- half teaspoonful paprika
- half teaspoonful cayenne pepper (adjust to taste)
- four cupful vegetable broth
- Salt and pepper to taste

Instructions:

1. Combine all ingredients in the Crockpot.
2. Stir well to ensure even distribution of spices.
3. Cook on low for six-eight hours.
4. Serve with your favorite toppings, such as sour cream, shredded cheese, and chopped green onions.

Duration for this recipe: six-eight hours on low

Nutrients (per portion):

- Caloric content: 300
- Amino content: 15g
- Carb content: 60g
- Fatty acid: 2g

2. CROCKPOT RED BEANS AND RICE

Servings: 8-10
Ingredients:
- one cupful dried red kidney beans, soaked and drained
- one onion, diced
- one bell pepper, diced
- three cloves garlic, minced
- one pound andouille sausage, sliced
- two cupful chicken broth
- one teaspoonful Cajun seasoning
- half teaspoonful thyme
- one-fourth teaspoonful cayenne pepper (adjust to taste)
- four cupful cooked white rice
- Salt and pepper to taste

Instructions:
1. Combine soaked red beans, onion, bell pepper, garlic, and andouille sausage in the Crockpot.
2. Add chicken broth and season with Cajun seasoning, thyme, and cayenne pepper.
3. Cook on low for seven-nine hours until beans are tender.
4. Serve over cooked white rice.

Duration for this recipe: seven-nine hours on low
Nutrients (per portion): Caloric content: 400, Amino content: 18g, Carb content: 40g, Fatty acid: 20g

3. CROCKPOT LENTIL AND BROWN RICE SOUP

Servings: 4-6
Ingredients:
- one cupful brown lentils, rinsed and drained
- one cupful brown rice
- one onion, diced
- two carrots, diced
- two celery stalks, diced
- three cloves garlic, minced
- six cupful vegetable broth
- one teaspoonful cumin
- half teaspoonful paprika
- half teaspoonful thyme
- Salt and pepper to taste

Instructions:
1. Combine lentils, brown rice, onion, carrots, celery, and garlic in the Crockpot.
2. Add vegetable broth and season with cumin, paprika, thyme, salt, and pepper.
3. Cook on low for seven-nine hours until lentils and rice are tender.
4. Adjust seasoning if needed before serving.

Duration for this recipe: seven-nine hours on low
Nutrients (per portion): Caloric content: 250, Amino content: 12g, Carb content: 50g, Fatty acid: 2g

4. CROCKPOT QUINOA AND BLACK BEAN STEW

Servings: 2-3
Ingredients:
- one cupful quinoa, rinsed
- one can (fifteen oz) black beans, drained and rinsed
- one can (fifteen oz) diced tomatoes
- one onion, diced
- one bell pepper, diced
- two cloves garlic, minced
- four cupful vegetable broth
- one teaspoonful chili powder
- half teaspoonful cumin
- half teaspoonful paprika
- Salt and pepper to taste

Instructions:
1. Combine quinoa, black beans, diced tomatoes, onion, bell pepper, and garlic in the Crockpot.
2. Add vegetable broth and season with chili powder, cumin, paprika, salt, and pepper.
3. Cook on low for four-six hours.
4. Serve as a hearty stew.

Duration for this recipe: four-six hours on low
Nutrients (per portion):
- Caloric content: 320
- Amino content: 12g
- Carb content: 60g
- Fatty acid: 3g

5. CROCKPOT WILD RICE AND MUSHROOM PILAF

Servings: 2-3
Ingredients:
- one cupful wild rice
- one cupful brown rice
- eight oz mushrooms, sliced
- one onion, diced
- three cloves garlic, minced
- four cupful vegetable broth
- half teaspoonful thyme
- half teaspoonful rosemary
- Salt and pepper to taste

Instructions:
1. Combine wild rice, brown rice, mushrooms, onion, and garlic in the Crockpot.
2. Add vegetable broth and season with thyme, rosemary, salt, and pepper.
3. Cook on low for six-eight hours until rice is tender.
4. Fluff with a fork before serving.

Duration for this recipe: six-eight hours on low
Nutrients (per portion):
- Caloric content: 250
- Amino content: 6g
- Carb content: 50g
- Fatty acid: 2g

6. CROCKPOT MEXICAN QUINOA BOWL

Servings: 2-3
Ingredients:
- one cupful quinoa, rinsed
- one can (fifteen oz) black beans, drained and rinsed
- one cupful corn kernels
- one bell pepper, diced
- one onion, diced
- one can (fifteen oz) diced tomatoes
- one teaspoonful chili powder
- half teaspoonful cumin
- half teaspoonful paprika
- four cupful vegetable broth
- Salt and pepper to taste

Instructions:
1. Combine quinoa, black beans, corn kernels, bell pepper, onion, and diced tomatoes in the Crockpot.
2. Add vegetable broth and season with chili powder, cumin, paprika, salt, and pepper.
3. Cook on low for four-six hours.
4. Serve as a flavorful Mexican quinoa bowl.

Duration for this recipe: four-six hours on low
Nutrients (per portion):
- Caloric content: 280
- Amino content: 10g
- Carb content: 50g
- Fatty acid: 3g

7. CROCKPOT ITALIAN FARRO AND VEGETABLE SOUP

Servings: 4-6
Ingredients:
- one cupful farro
- two carrots, diced
- two celery stalks, diced
- one zucchini, diced
- one onion, diced
- two cloves garlic, minced
- one can (fifteen oz) diced tomatoes
- eight cupful vegetable broth
- one teaspoonful Italian seasoning
- Salt and pepper to taste

Instructions:
1. Combine farro, carrots, celery, zucchini, onion, garlic, and diced tomatoes in the Crockpot.
2. Add vegetable broth and season with Italian seasoning, salt, and pepper.
3. Cook on low for seven-nine hours.
4. Serve as a comforting Italian farro and vegetable soup.

Duration for this recipe: seven-nine hours on low
Nutrients (per portion): Caloric content: 220
- Amino content: 6g
- Carb content: 45g
- Fatty acid: 1g

8. CROCKPOT CHICKPEA AND SPINACH CURRY

Servings: 2-3

Ingredients:
- two cans (fifteen oz each) chickpeas, drained and rinsed
- one onion, diced
- two cloves garlic, minced
- one tbsp ginger
- one can (fifteen oz) diced tomatoes
- one can (fifteen oz) coconut milk
- two cupful fresh spinach
- two tablespoonful curry powder
- one teaspoonful cumin
- one Tbsp honey
- half teaspoonful paprika
- Salt and pepper to taste

Instructions:

1. Pour the oil into a frying pan and set it on medium heat, and cook the onions, garlic, and ginger until they become tender.

2. Transfer the sautéed onion mix into a blender, add coconut milk, honey and all the spices and salt. blend everything until it reaches a smooth consistency.

3. Puti in into the crock pot and add the chickpeas.

4. Cook on low for four-six hours.

5. Serve with rice or naan bread.

Duration for this recipe: four-six hours on low

Nutrients (per portion): Caloric content: 350, Amino content: 10g, Carb content: 35g, Fatty acid: 20g

9. CROCKPOT BARLEY AND VEGETABLE STEW

Servings: 4-6

Ingredients:
- one cupful pearl barley
- two carrots, diced
- two potatoes, diced
- one onion, diced
- two cloves garlic, minced
- four cupful vegetable broth
- one teaspoonful thyme
- half teaspoonful rosemary
- Salt and pepper to taste

Instructions:

1. Combine pearl barley, carrots, potatoes, onion, and garlic in the Crockpot.

2. Add vegetable broth and season with thyme, rosemary, salt, and pepper.

3. Cook on low for seven-nine hours.

4. Serve as a hearty barley and vegetable stew.

Duration for this recipe: seven-nine hours on low

Nutrients (per portion): Caloric content: 280, Amino content: 6g, Carb content: 60g, Fatty acid: 1g

10. CROCKPOT MEXICAN RICE AND BLACK BEANS

Servings: 2-4
- one cupful white rice
- one can (15 oz) black beans, drained and rinsed
- one bell pepper, diced
- one onion, diced
- two cloves garlic, minced
- one can (fifteen oz) diced tomatoes
- one teaspoonful chili powder
- half teaspoonful cumin
- half teaspoonful paprika
- two cupful vegetable broth
- Salt and pepper to taste

Instructions:

1. Combine white rice, black beans, bell pepper, onion, garlic, diced tomatoes, and vegetable broth in the Crockpot.

2. Season with chili powder, cumin, paprika, salt, and pepper.

3. Cook on low for four-six hours.

4. Serve as a flavorful Mexican rice and black bean dish.

Duration for this recipe: four-six hours on low

Nutrients (per portion): Caloric content: 250, Amino content: 6g, Carb content: 50g, Fatty acid: 1g

CHAPTER 9:
BEEF, PORK, LAMB

1. CROCKPOT BEEF STEW

Servings: 2-4

Ingredients:

- one and a half lbs beef stew meat, cubed
- four cupful beef broth
- two cloves garlic, minced
- Olive Oil
- four carrots, sliced
- four potatoes, diced
- one onion, chopped
- one cupful frozen peas
- one teaspoonful dried thyme
- one teaspoonful dried rosemary
- Salt and pepper to taste
- one-fourth cupful all-purpose flour

Instructions:

1. In a bowl, season the beef with salt, pepper, and all-purpose flour.
2. Place the seasoned beef, carrots, potatoes, onion, and garlic in the Crockpot.
3. Pour beef broth over the ingredients.
4. Add dried thyme and dried rosemary.
5. Stir to combine.
6. Cook on low for seven-eight hours or on high for four-five hours.
7. Add frozen peas in the last 30 minutes of cooking.
8. Serve hot.

Duration for this recipe: seven-eight hours on low, or four-five hours on high

Nutrients (per portion): Caloric content: 350, Amino content: 28g, Carb content: 35g, Fatty acid: 10g

2. CROCKPOT PULLED PORK

Servings: 2-3
- three lbs pork shoulder or butt roast
- one cupful barbecue sauce
- one-fourth cupful apple cider vinegar
- one-fourth cupful brown sugar
- one tablespoonful smoked paprika
- one tablespoonful garlic powder
- one tablespoonful onion powder
- Salt and pepper to taste

Instructions:
1. Season the pork roast with salt, pepper, smoked paprika, garlic powder, and onion powder.
2. Place the seasoned pork in the Crockpot.
3. In a bowl, mix together barbecue sauce, apple cider vinegar, and brown sugar.
4. Pour the sauce over the pork.
5. Cook on low for eight-ten hours or on high for four-six hours.
6. Shred the pork with two forks and stir in the sauce.
7. Serve on buns with coleslaw.

Duration for this recipe: eight-ten hours on low, or four-six hours on high

Nutrients (per portion, excluding buns and coleslaw):
- Caloric content: 320
- Amino content: 28g
- Carb content: 20g
- Fatty acid: 15g

3. CROCKPOT BEEF AND BROCCOLI

Servings: 4-6
Ingredients:
- one and a half lbs beef sirloin, thinly sliced
- one cupful beef broth
- half cupful low-sodium soy sauce
- one-fourth cupful brown sugar
- two cloves garlic, minced
- one tablespoonful sesame oil
- four cupful broccoli florets
- two tablespoonful cornstarch
- Cooked rice for serving

Instructions:
1. Place the sliced beef in the Crockpot.
2. In a bowl, whisk together beef broth, soy sauce, brown sugar, garlic, and sesame oil.
3. Pour the sauce over the beef.
4. Cook on low for four-five hours.
5. In the last 30 minutes of cooking, add broccoli florets.
6. In a small bowl, mix cornstarch with a couple of tablespoonful of water to create a slurry.
7. Stir the cornstarch slurry into the Crockpot to thicken the sauce.
8. Serve over cooked rice.

Duration for this recipe: four-five hours on low
Nutrients (per portion, excluding rice):
- Caloric content: 280
- Amino content: 26g
- Carb content: 16g
- Fatty acid: 12g

4. CROCKPOT PORK CARNITAS

Servings: 4-5
- 2-3 lbs pork shoulder, cut into chunks
- one onion, chopped
- three cloves garlic, minced
- 1/2 teaspoonful ground cumin
- ¼ teaspoon cinnamon
- 1/2 teaspoonful chili powder
- half teaspoonful dried oregano
- half teaspoonful salt
- 1/2 teaspoon black pepper
- Juice of one limes
- One quarter cupful orange juice
- Corn tortillas for serving
- 6 ounces of beer (Lager beer)

Instructions:
1. Place the pork chunks, chopped onion, and minced garlic in the Crockpot.
2. In a bowl, mix cumin, cinnamon, chili powder, dried oregano, salt, and black pepper.
3. Sprinkle the spice mixture over the pork.

4. Squeeze the lime juice and pour the orange juice and the beer over the pork.

5. Cook on low for six-eight hours.

6. Shred the pork with two forks.

7. Serve the carnitas in corn tortillas with your favorite toppings.

Duration for this recipe: six-eight hours on low

Nutrients (per portion, excluding tortillas and toppings):

- Caloric content: 280
- Amino content: 30g
- Carb content: 8g
- Fatty acid: 14g

5. CROCKPOT LAMB STEW

Servings: 8-10

Ingredients:

- one and a half lbs boneless lamb stew meat
- four cupful beef broth
- four carrots, sliced
- four potatoes, diced
- one onion, chopped
- two cloves garlic, minced
- one cupful frozen peas
- one teaspoonful dried thyme
- one teaspoonful dried rosemary
- Salt and pepper to taste
- one-fourth cupful all-purpose flour

Instructions:

1. In a bowl, season the lamb with salt, pepper, and all-purpose flour.

2. Place the seasoned lamb, carrots, potatoes, chopped onion, and minced garlic in the Crockpot.

3. Pour beef broth over the ingredients.

4. Add dried thyme and dried rosemary.

5. Stir to combine.

6. Cook on low for seven-eight hours or on high for four-five hours.

7. Add frozen peas in the last 30 minutes of cooking.

8. Serve hot.

Duration for this recipe: seven-eight hours on low, or four-five hours on high

Nutrients (per portion):

- Caloric content: 320
- Amino content: 28g
- Carb content: 35g
- Fatty acid: 10g
-

6. CROCKPOT BBQ PORK RIBS

Servings: 2-4

Ingredients:

For the sauce:

- one cupful barbecue sauce
- one tablespoonful smoked paprika
- 5/4 Worcestershire sauce
- one tablespoonful garlic powder
- one tablespoonful onion powder

For the Pork ribs:

- three lbs pork baby back ribs
- one-fourth cupful apple cider vinegar
- one-fourth cupful brown sugar
- Salt and pepper to taste

Instructions:

1. Season the ribs with salt, pepper, smoked paprika, Worcestershire sauce, garlic powder, and onion powder.

2. Place the seasoned ribs in the Crockpot, standing up along the walls.

3. In a bowl, mix together barbecue sauce, apple cider vinegar, and brown sugar.

4. Pour the sauce over the ribs.

5. Cook on low for six-eight hours.

6. Carefully remove the ribs from the Crockpot.

7. Brush with additional barbecue sauce and grill or broil for a few minutes for a caramelized finish.

8. Serve hot.

Duration for this recipe: six-eight hours on low

Nutrients (per portion):

- Caloric content: 350
- Amino content: 28g
- Carb content: 20g
- Fatty acid: 16g

7. CROCKPOT BEEF AND BARLEY STEW

Servings: 2-3
Ingredients:

- one and a half lbs beef stew meat, cubed
- four cupful beef broth
- four carrots, sliced
- two potatoes, diced
- one onion, chopped
- two cloves garlic, minced
- one cupful pearl barley
- Worcester sauce
- one teaspoonful dried thyme
- one teaspoonful dried rosemary
- Salt and pepper to taste

Instructions:

1. In a bowl, season the beef with salt, pepper, dried thyme, and dried rosemary.
2. Place the seasoned beef, carrots, potatoes, chopped onion, Worcester sauce and minced garlic in the Crockpot.
3. Add beef broth and pearl barley.
4. Stir well to combine all ingredients.
5. Cook on low for seven-eight hours or on high for four-five hours.
6. Serve hot.

Duration for this recipe: seven-eight hours on low, or four-five hours on high

Nutrients (per portion):

- Caloric content: 320
- Amino content: 30g
- Carb content: 35g
- Fatty acid: 8g

8. CROCKPOT PORK AND SAUERKRAUT

Servings: 5-7
Ingredients:

- two lbs boneless pork loin roast
- one lb sauerkraut, drained and rinsed
- two baking apples, sliced
- one onion, chopped
- one-fourth cupful brown sugar
- half teaspoonful caraway seeds
- 3 1/3 butter
- Salt and pepper to taste

Instructions:

1. Season the pork roast with salt and pepper.
2. Place the seasoned pork in the Crockpot.
3. Add sliced apples, chopped onion, brown sugar, caraway seeds and sauerkraut last on top.
4. Cook on low for six-eight hours.
5. Melt the butter in a bain-marie and pour it on top
6. Serve with mashed potatoes or rye bread.

Duration for this recipe: six-eight hours on low

Nutrients (per portion):

- Caloric content: 280
- Amino content: 26g
- Carb content: 20g
- Fatty acid: 10g

9. CROCKPOT LAMB ROGAN JOSH

Servings: 7-9
Ingredients:

- one and a half lbs boneless lamb stew meat
- one onion, chopped
- two cloves garlic, minced
- one-inch piece of ginger, minced
- one can (fourteen oz) diced tomatoes
- half cupful plain yogurt
- two teaspoonful ground coriander
- two teaspoonful ground cumin
- one teaspoonful paprika
- half teaspoonful cayenne pepper (adjust to taste)
- Salt and pepper to taste
- Fresh cilantro for garnish

Instructions:

1. Place the lamb, chopped onion, minced garlic, and minced ginger in the Crockpot.
2. In a bowl, mix together diced tomatoes, plain yogurt, ground coriander, ground cumin, paprika, cayenne pepper, salt, and pepper.
3. Pour the tomato-yogurt mixture over the lamb.
4. Cook on low for six-eight hours.

5. Serve with steamed rice or naan bread and garnish with fresh cilantro.

Duration for this recipe: six-eight hours on low
Nutrients (per portion, excluding rice or naan):
- Caloric content: 320
- Amino content: 26g
- Carb content: 12g
- Fatty acid: 18g

10. CROCKPOT PORK AND BEAN CASSEROLE

Servings: 2-3

Ingredients:
- two lbs pork tenderloin, cubed
- two cans (fifteen oz each) of baked beans
- one onion, chopped
- one green bell pepper, diced
- half cupful barbecue sauce
- one-fourth cupful brown sugar
- two tablespoonful mustard
- half teaspoonful garlic powder
- Salt and pepper to taste

Instructions:
1. In a bowl, season the pork with salt, pepper, and garlic powder.
2. Place the seasoned pork in the Crockpot.
3. Add baked beans, chopped onion, diced bell pepper, barbecue sauce, brown sugar, and mustard.
4. Stir well to combine all ingredients.
5. Cook on low for six-eight hours.
6. Serve hot.

Duration for this recipe: six-eight hours on low
Nutrients (per portion):
- Caloric content: 350
- Amino content: 32g
- Carb content: 45g
- Fatty acid: 6g

CHAPTER 10:
POULTRY

1. CROCKPOT CHICKEN AND RICE SOUP

Servings: 6-7

Ingredients:

- one lb boneless, skinless chicken breasts, cubed
- 1 tbsp of salted butter
- one cupful carrots, sliced
- one cupful celery, chopped
- one cupful onion, chopped
- two cloves garlic, minced
- one cupful long-grain white rice
- six cupful chicken broth
- one teaspoonful dried thyme
- one bay leaf
- 1 ½ instantaneous rice
- Salt and pepper to taste
- Fresh parsley for garnish

Instructions:

1. First, we cook the butter and onion in a separate small frying pan.
2. Place chicken, carrots, celery, onion, and garlic in the Crockpot.
3. Add rice, chicken broth, dried thyme, bay leaf, salt, and pepper.
4. Stir to combine all ingredients.
5. Cook on low for six-eight hours or on high for three-four hours.
6. Add the instant rice about ten minutes before the end of cooking, or before serving.
7. Remove the bay leaf before serving.
8. Garnish with fresh parsley.

Duration for this recipe: six-eight hours on low, or three-four hours on high

Nutrients (per portion):

- Caloric content: 280
- Amino content: 22g
- Carb content: 35g
- Fatty acid: 4g

2. CROCKPOT BBQ PULLED CHICKEN

Servings: 3-5

Ingredients:

- two lbs boneless, skinless chicken breasts
- one cupful barbecue sauce
- one-fourth cupful apple cider vinegar
- one-fourth cupful brown sugar
- one tablespoonful Worcestershire sauce
- one teaspoonful smoked paprika
- half teaspoonful garlic powder
- half teaspoonful onion powder
- Salt and pepper to taste

Instructions:

1. Place chicken breasts in the Crockpot.
2. In a bowl, mix together barbecue sauce, apple cider vinegar, brown sugar, Worcestershire sauce, smoked paprika, garlic powder, onion powder, salt, and pepper.
3. Pour the sauce over the chicken.
4. Cook on low for six-eight hours or on high for three-four hours.
5. Shred the chicken with two forks and stir in the sauce.
6. Serve on buns with coleslaw.

Duration for this recipe: six-eight hours on low, or three-four hours on high

Nutrients (per portion, excluding buns and coleslaw):

- Caloric content: 280
- Amino content: 28g
- Carb content: 20g
- Fatty acid: 8g

3. CROCKPOT CHICKEN TIKKA MASALA

Servings: 2-3

Ingredients:

- two lbs boneless, skinless chicken thighs, cubed
- one onion, chopped
- four cloves garlic, minced
- one-inch piece of ginger, minced
- one can (fourteen oz) diced tomatoes
- half cupful tomato sauce
- one cupful heavy cream
- two tablespoonful garam masala
- one tablespoonful paprika
- one teaspoonful turmeric
- Salt and pepper to taste
- Fresh cilantro for garnish
- Cooked rice for serving

Instructions:

1. Place chicken, chopped onion, minced garlic, and minced ginger in the Crockpot.
2. In a bowl, mix diced tomatoes, tomato sauce, heavy cream, garam masala, paprika, turmeric, salt, and pepper.
3. Pour the sauce over the chicken.
4. Cook on low for six-eight hours.
5. Serve over cooked rice and garnish with fresh cilantro.

Duration for this recipe: six-eight hours on low

Nutrients (per portion, excluding rice):

- Caloric content: 350
- Amino content: 28g
- Carb content: 10g
- Fatty acid: 20g

4. CROCKPOT TURKEY CHILI

Servings: 8-10

Ingredients:

- one lb ground turkey
- one onion, chopped
- two cloves garlic, minced
- one can (fifteen oz) kidney beans, drained and rinsed

- one can (fifteen oz) black beans, drained and rinsed
- one can (fifteen oz) diced tomatoes
- one can (fifteen oz) tomato sauce
- one cupful corn kernels (frozen or canned)
- two tablespoonful chili powder
- one teaspoonful cumin
- Salt and pepper to taste
- Shredded cheddar cheese and chopped green onions for garnish

Instructions:

1. In a skillet, brown ground turkey with chopped onion and minced garlic. Drain excess fat.

2. Place the cooked turkey mixture in the Crockpot.

3. Add kidney beans, black beans, diced tomatoes, tomato sauce, corn kernels, chili powder, cumin, salt, and pepper.

4. Stir to combine all ingredients.

5. Cook on low for six-eight hours.

6. Serve with shredded cheddar cheese and chopped green onions.

Duration for this recipe: six-eight hours on low

Nutrients (per portion, excluding garnishes):

- Caloric content: 280
- Amino content: 22g
- Carb content: 35g
- Fatty acid: 6g

5. CROCKPOT LEMON GARLIC CHICKEN

Servings: 2-3

- four boneless, skinless chicken breasts
- one-fourth cupful chicken broth
- Juice of two lemons
- four cloves garlic, minced
- one teaspoonful dried oregano
- half teaspoonful dried thyme
- Salt and pepper to taste
- Fresh parsley for garnish

Instructions:

1. Place chicken breasts in the Crockpot.

2. In a bowl, mix chicken broth, lemon juice, minced garlic, dried oregano, dried thyme, salt, and pepper.

3. Pour the mixture over the chicken.

4. Cook on low for four-six hours.

5. Garnish with fresh parsley before serving.

6. Serve with your favorite side dishes.

Duration for this recipe: four-six hours on low

Nutrients (per portion, excluding side dishes):

- Caloric content: 180
- Amino content: 30g
- Carb content: 4g
- Fatty acid: 4g

6. CROCKPOT CHICKEN ENCHILADA CASSEROLE

Servings: 2-4

- one and a half lbs boneless, skinless chicken breasts, cubed
- one can (ten oz) red enchilada sauce
- one can (four oz) green chilies
- one onion, chopped
- two cloves garlic, minced
- two cupful shredded cheddar cheese
- eight small corn tortillas
- Sliced olives, diced tomatoes, and chopped cilantro for garnish

Instructions:

1. Place chicken, red enchilada sauce, green chilies, chopped onion, and minced garlic in the Crockpot.

2. Layer corn tortillas on top of the mixture.

3. Sprinkle shredded cheddar cheese on the tortillas.

4. Repeat the layers.

5. Cook on low for six-eight hours.

6. Garnish with sliced olives, diced tomatoes, and chopped cilantro before serving.

Duration for this recipe: six-eight hours on low

Nutrients (per portion):

- Caloric content: 320
- Amino content: 28g
- Carb content: 20g

- Fatty acid: 14g

7. CROCKPOT TERIYAKI CHICKEN

Servings: 2-3
- two lbs boneless, skinless chicken thighs
- half cupful low-sodium soy sauce
- one-fourth cupful honey
- one-fourth cupful rice vinegar
- one-fourth cupful water
- two cloves garlic, minced
- one tablespoonful fresh ginger, grated
- half teaspoonful red pepper flakes (adjust to taste)
- Sesame seeds and green onions for garnish
- Cooked rice for serving

Instructions:
1. Place chicken thighs in the Crockpot.
2. In a bowl, mix soy sauce, honey, rice vinegar, water, minced garlic, grated ginger, and red pepper flakes.
3. Pour the sauce over the chicken.
4. Cook on low for four-six hours.
5. Garnish with sesame seeds and chopped green onions.
6. Serve over cooked rice.

Duration for this recipe: four-six hours on low
Nutrients (per portion, excluding rice):
- Caloric content: 320
- Amino content: 30g
- Carb content: 25g
- Fatty acid: 10g

8. CROCKPOT TURKEY MEATBALLS

Servings: 2-3
Ingredients:
- one lb ground turkey
- one-fourth cupful breadcrumbs
- one-fourth cupful grated Parmesan cheese
- one egg
- one-fourth cupful milk
- one-fourth cupful fresh parsley, chopped
- one clove garlic, minced
- half teaspoonful dried oregano
- half teaspoonful dried basil
- one can (fourteen oz) crushed tomatoes
- one-fourth cupful tomato sauce
- half teaspoonful red pepper flakes (adjust to taste)
- Salt and pepper to taste

Instructions:
1. In a bowl, combine ground turkey, breadcrumbs, grated Parmesan cheese, egg, milk, chopped parsley, minced garlic, dried oregano, dried basil, salt, and pepper.
2. Shape the mixture into meatballs and place them in the Crockpot.
3. In another bowl, mix crushed tomatoes, tomato sauce, and red pepper flakes.
4. Pour the tomato mixture over the meatballs.
5. Cook on low for four-six hours.
6. Serve with pasta or as a sandwich.

Duration for this recipe: four-six hours on low
Nutrients (per portion, excluding pasta or bread):
- Caloric content: 280
- Amino content: 28g
- Carb content: 15g
- Fatty acid: 12g

9. CROCKPOT CHICKEN FAJITAS

Servings: 4-6
Ingredients:
- one and a half lbs boneless, skinless chicken breasts, sliced
- one onion, sliced
- one red bell pepper, sliced
- one green bell pepper, sliced
- Ten Oz. can Ro-tel tomatoes & green chili
- half teaspoonful garlic powder
- Salt and pepper to taste
- Flour tortillas for serving
- Sliced avocado, sour cream, and shredded cheese for garnish

Instructions:
1. Mix the honey, garlic and Ro-tel in a bowl. Finally pour into the bottom of the crock pot .

2. Place chicken slices, sliced onion, sliced red bell pepper, and sliced green bell pepper in the Crockpot.

3. Add diced tomatoes, salt, and pepper.

4. Stir to combine all ingredients.

5. Cook on low for four-six hours.

6. Serve in flour tortillas with sliced avocado, sour cream, and shredded cheese.

Duration for this recipe: four-six hours on low

Nutrients (per portion, excluding tortillas and garnishes):

- Caloric content: 280
- Amino content: 26g
- Carb content: 15g
- Fatty acid: 10g

3. Add diced tomatoes, coconut milk, curry powder, ground cumin, ground coriander, turmeric, red pepper flakes, salt, and pepper.

4. Stir to combine all ingredients.

5. Cook on low for four-six hours.

6. Serve over cooked rice and garnish with fresh cilantro.

Duration for this recipe: four-six hours on low

Nutrients (per portion, excluding rice):

- Caloric content: 320
- Amino content: 24g
- Carb content: 10g
- Fatty acid: 22g

10. CROCKPOT TURKEY AND VEGETABLE CURRY

Servings: 2-3

Ingredients:

- one lb ground turkey
- one onion, chopped
- two cloves garlic, minced
- one red bell pepper, chopped
- one zucchini, chopped
- one can (fourteen oz) diced tomatoes
- one can (fourteen oz) coconut milk
- two tablespoonful curry powder
- one teaspoonful ground cumin
- half teaspoonful ground coriander
- half teaspoonful turmeric
- half teaspoonful red pepper flakes (adjust to taste)
- Salt and pepper to taste
- Fresh cilantro for garnish
- Cooked rice for serving

Instructions:

1. In a skillet, brown ground turkey with chopped onion and minced garlic. Drain excess fat.

2. Place the cooked turkey mixture, chopped red bell pepper, and chopped zucchini in the Crockpot.

50

CHAPTER 11:
FISH AND SEAFOOD

1. CROCKPOT LEMON GARLIC SHRIMP

Servings: 2-3
- one lb large shrimp, peeled and deveined
- four cloves garlic, minced
- Juice of two lemons
- one-fourth cupful chicken broth
- one-fourth cupful white wine (optional)
- one-fourth cupful unsalted butter, melted
- one-fourth cupful fresh parsley, chopped
- Salt and pepper to taste
- Cooked pasta or rice for serving

Instructions:

1. Place shrimp and minced garlic in the Crockpot.

2. In a bowl, mix lemon juice, chicken broth, white wine (if using), melted butter, chopped parsley, salt, and pepper.

3. Pour the mixture over the shrimp.

4. Cook on low for one-two hours, just until the shrimp turn pink.

5. Serve over cooked pasta or rice.

Duration for this recipe: one-two hours on low
Nutrients (per portion, excluding pasta or rice):
- Caloric content: 200
- Amino content: 18g
- Carb content: 4g
- Fatty acid: 12g

2. CROCKPOT CLAM CHOWDER

Servings: 2-3
Ingredients:
- two cans (ten oz each) minced clams, with juice
- four cupful potatoes, diced

- one onion, chopped
- two cloves garlic, minced
- three cupful chicken broth
- one cupful heavy cream
- one-fourth cupful all-purpose flour
- four slices bacon, cooked and crumbled
- one teaspoonful dried thyme
- Salt and pepper to taste

Instructions:

1. In the Crockpot, combine minced clams with their juice, diced potatoes, chopped onion, minced garlic, chicken broth, heavy cream, all-purpose flour, crumbled bacon, dried thyme, salt, and pepper.
2. Stir well to combine all ingredients.
3. Cook on low for four-six hours.
4. Serve hot with crusty bread.

Duration for this recipe: four-six hours on low
Nutrients (per portion, excluding bread):
- Caloric content: 280
- Amino content: 10g
- Carb content: 30g
- Fatty acid: 14g

3. CROCKPOT COCONUT CURRY SALMON

Servings: 5-7
Ingredients:
- four salmon fillets
- one can (fourteen oz) coconut milk
- two tablespoonful red curry paste
- one red bell pepper, sliced
- one zucchini, sliced
- one cupful snap peas
- one teaspoonful ginger, minced
- one clove garlic, minced
- one tablespoonful fish sauce
- Juice of one lime
- Fresh cilantro for garnish
- Cooked rice for serving

Instructions:

1. Place salmon fillets in the Crockpot.

2. In a bowl, whisk together coconut milk, red curry paste, sliced red bell pepper, sliced zucchini, snap peas, minced ginger, minced garlic, fish sauce, and lime juice.
3. Pour the mixture over the salmon.
4. Cook on low for two-three hours, just until the salmon flakes easily.
5. Garnish with fresh cilantro and serve over cooked rice.

Duration for this recipe: two-three hours on low
Nutrients (per portion, excluding rice):
- Caloric content: 300
- Amino content: 25g
- Carb content: 10g
- Fatty acid: 18g

4. CROCKPOT SHRIMP AND CRAB GUMBO

Servings: 3-6
Ingredients:
- one lb large shrimp, peeled and deveined
- eight oz crab meat
- one onion, chopped
- one green bell pepper, chopped
- one red bell pepper, chopped
- two celery stalks, chopped
- four cloves garlic, minced
- one can (fourteen oz) diced tomatoes
- four cupful chicken broth
- two bay leaves
- one tablespoonful gumbo file powder
- one teaspoonful dried thyme
- half teaspoonful cayenne pepper (adjust to taste)
- Salt and pepper to taste
- Cooked rice for serving

Instructions:

1. Place shrimp, crab meat, chopped onion, chopped green and red bell peppers, chopped celery, minced garlic, diced tomatoes, chicken broth, bay leaves, gumbo file powder, dried thyme, cayenne pepper, salt, and pepper in the Crockpot.
2. Stir to combine all ingredients.

3. Cook on low for four-six hours.

4. Serve over cooked rice.

Duration for this recipe: four-six hours on low

Nutrients (per portion, excluding rice):

- Caloric content: 280
- Amino content: 28g
- Carb content: 20g
- Fatty acid: 10g

5. CROCKPOT TUNA NOODLE CASSEROLE

Servings: 6-9

Ingredients:

- eight oz egg noodles, cooked and drained
- two cans (five oz each) tuna, drained
- one cupful frozen peas
- one cupful sliced mushrooms
- half cupful mayonnaise
- half cupful sour cream
- one cupful shredded cheddar cheese
- one-fourth cupful grated Parmesan cheese
- one teaspoonful garlic powder
- Salt and pepper to taste
- Crushed potato chips for topping

Instructions:

1. In the Crockpot, combine cooked and drained egg noodles, drained tuna, frozen peas, sliced mushrooms, mayonnaise, sour cream, shredded cheddar cheese, grated Parmesan cheese, garlic powder, salt, and pepper.

2. Stir well to combine all ingredients.

3. Top with crushed potato chips.

4. Cook on low for two-three hours.

5. Serve hot.

Duration for this recipe: two-three hours on low

Nutrients (per portion):

- Caloric content: 350
- Amino content: 20g
- Carb content: 25g
- Fatty acid: 20g

6. CROCKPOT SEAFOOD PAELLA

Servings: 2-3

Ingredients:

- one cupful Arborio rice
- one lb large shrimp, peeled and deveined
- one lb mussels, cleaned and debearded
- half lb squid, cleaned and sliced
- one onion, chopped
- one red bell pepper, chopped
- one green bell pepper, chopped
- two cloves garlic, minced
- one can (fourteen oz) diced tomatoes
- two cupful chicken broth
- one teaspoonful saffron threads (optional)
- one teaspoonful paprika
- half teaspoonful cayenne pepper (adjust to taste)
- Salt and pepper to taste
- Fresh parsley for garnish

Instructions:

1. In the Crockpot, combine Arborio rice, large shrimp, mussels, sliced squid, chopped onion, chopped red and green bell peppers, minced garlic, diced tomatoes, chicken broth, saffron threads (if using), paprika, cayenne pepper, salt, and pepper.

2. Stir well to combine all ingredients.

3. Cook on low for two-three hours, or until the rice is tender and the seafood is cooked.

4. Garnish with fresh parsley and serve.

Duration for this recipe: two-three hours on low

Nutrients (per portion):

- Caloric content: 350
- Amino content: 30g
- Carb content: 35g
- Fatty acid: 10g

7. CROCKPOT SALMON WITH DILL SAUCE

Servings: 4-6

- four salmon fillets
- half cupful chicken broth
- half cupful dry white wine

- two tablespoonful fresh dill, chopped
- one-fourth cupful sour cream
- one-fourth cupful mayonnaise
- Juice of one lemon
- Salt and pepper to taste

Instructions:

1. Place salmon fillets in the Crockpot.

2. In a bowl, mix chicken broth, white wine, chopped dill, sour cream, mayonnaise, lemon juice, salt, and pepper.

3. Pour the mixture over the salmon.

4. Cook on low for two-three hours, just until the salmon flakes easily.

5. Serve with additional dill sauce.

Duration for this recipe: two-three hours on low
Nutrients (per portion, excluding additional sauce):

- Caloric content: 300
- Amino content: 30g
- Carb content: 4g
- Fatty acid: 18g

8. CROCKPOT GARLIC BUTTER SCALLOPS

Servings: 2-3

Ingredients:

- one lb large sea scallops
- four cloves garlic, minced
- one-fourth cupful unsalted butter, melted
- Juice of one lemon
- one-fourth cupful white wine
- one-fourth cupful chicken broth
- Salt and pepper to taste
- Fresh parsley for garnish
- Cooked pasta or rice for serving

Instructions:

1. Place sea scallops in the Crockpot.

2. In a bowl, combine minced garlic, melted butter, lemon juice, white wine, chicken broth, salt, and pepper.

3. Pour the mixture over the scallops.

4. Cook on low for one-two hours, just until the scallops are opaque.

5. Garnish with fresh parsley and serve over cooked pasta or rice.

Duration for this recipe: one-two hours on low
Nutrients (per portion, excluding pasta or rice):

- Caloric content: 200
- Amino content: 18g
- Carb content: 4g
- Fatty acid: 12g

9. CROCKPOT CRAB AND CORN CHOWDER

Servings: 8-10

Ingredients:

- eight oz crab meat
- two cupful corn kernels (fresh or frozen)
- one onion, chopped
- two potatoes, diced
- four cupful chicken broth
- one cupful heavy cream
- one-fourth cupful all-purpose flour
- two tablespoonful butter
- half teaspoonful Old Bay seasoning
- Salt and pepper to taste
- Cooked bacon bits for garnish

Instructions:

1. In the Crockpot, combine crab meat, corn kernels, chopped onion, diced potatoes, chicken broth, heavy cream, all-purpose flour, butter, Old Bay seasoning, salt, and pepper.

2. Stir well to combine all ingredients.

3. Cook on low for four-six hours.

4. Garnish with cooked bacon bits and serve.

Duration for this recipe: four-six hours on low
Nutrients (per portion, excluding bacon bits):

- Caloric content: 280
- Amino content: 16g
- Carb content: 25g
- Fatty acid: 14g

10. CROCKPOT COD WITH TOMATO AND OLIVES

Servings: 2-6

Ingredients:

- four cod fillets
- one can (fourteen oz) diced tomatoes
- half cupful Kalamata olives, pitted and sliced
- one onion, chopped
- two cloves garlic, minced
- one-fourth cupful fresh basil, chopped
- one-fourth cupful fresh parsley, chopped
- one-fourth cupful dry white wine
- Salt and pepper to taste
- Cooked quinoa or couscous for serving

Instructions:

1. Place cod fillets in the Crockpot.
2. In a bowl, combine diced tomatoes, sliced Kalamata olives, chopped onion, minced garlic, chopped basil, chopped parsley, dry white wine, salt, and pepper.
3. Pour the mixture over the cod.
4. Cook on low for two-three hours, just until the cod flakes easily.
5. Serve over cooked quinoa or couscous.

Duration for this recipe: two-three hours on low

Nutrients (per portion, excluding quinoa or couscous):

- Caloric content: 240
- Amino content: 30g
- Carb content: 10g
- Fatty acid: 8g

CHAPTER 12:
DESSERT

1. CROCKPOT APPLE CRISP

Servings: 2-4
Ingredients:
- six cupful apples, peeled, cored, and sliced
- half cupful granulated sugar
- one teaspoonful ground cinnamon
- half teaspoonful ground nutmeg
- half cupful old-fashioned oats
- half cupful all-purpose flour
- half cupful brown sugar
- one-fourth cupful unsalted butter, softened
- Vanilla ice cream (for serving)

Instructions:
1. In the Crockpot, combine sliced apples, granulated sugar, cinnamon, and nutmeg.
2. In a separate bowl, mix oats, flour, brown sugar, and softened butter until crumbly.

3. Sprinkle the oat mixture over the apples in the Crockpot.
4. Cover and cook on low for three-four hours.
5. Serve warm with a scoop of vanilla ice cream.
Duration for this recipe: three-four hours on low
Nutrients (per portion, excluding ice cream):
- Caloric content: 280
- Amino content: 2g
- Carb content: 65g
- Fatty acid: 5g

2. CROCKPOT CHOCOLATE LAVA CAKE

Servings: 2-3
Ingredients:
- one cupful all-purpose flour
- 3/four cupful granulated sugar

- two tablespoonful unsweetened cocoa powder
- two teaspoonful baking powder
- one-fourth teaspoonful salt
- half cupful milk
- two tablespoonful vegetable oil
- one teaspoonful vanilla extract
- half cupful semisweet chocolate chips
- half cupful chopped walnuts (optional)
- one cupful boiling water

Instructions:

1. In the Crockpot, whisk together flour, half cupful granulated sugar, cocoa powder, baking powder, and salt.

2. Stir in milk, vegetable oil, and vanilla extract until smooth.

3. Add chocolate chips and walnuts (if using) and spread evenly.

4. In a separate bowl, combine the remaining one-fourth cupful granulated sugar and boiling water. Pour this mixture over the batter in the Crockpot.

5. Cover and cook on low for two-three hours. The cake will rise to the top, and a rich, gooey chocolate sauce will form at the bottom.

6. Serve warm, and scoop some of the sauce over each serving.

Duration for this recipe: two-three hours on low
Nutrients (per portion): Caloric content: 320, Amino content: 4g, Carb content: 50g, Fatty acid: 12g

3. CROCKPOT BREAD PUDDING

Servings: 4-6
Ingredients:
- six cupful day-old bread cubes
- two cupful milk
- half cupful granulated sugar
- two eggs
- one-fourth cupful unsalted butter, melted
- one teaspoonful vanilla extract
- half cupful raisins (optional)
- half teaspoonful ground cinnamon

- one-fourth teaspoonful ground nutmeg
- Whipped cream (for serving)

Instructions:

1. In the Crockpot, combine bread cubes and milk. Let it soak for about fifteen minutes.

2. In a bowl, whisk together sugar, eggs, melted butter, vanilla extract, raisins (if using), ground cinnamon, and ground nutmeg.

3. Pour the egg mixture over the soaked bread cubes in the Crockpot.

4. Cover and cook on low for two-three hours, until the pudding is set.

5. Serve warm, topped with whipped cream.

Duration for this recipe: two-three hours on low
Nutrients (per portion, excluding whipped cream):
- Caloric content: 280
- Amino content: 6g
- Carb content: 45g
- Fatty acid: 9g

4. CROCKPOT RICE PUDDING

Servings: 2-3
- one cupful long-grain white rice
- four cupful whole milk
- half cupful granulated sugar
- two teaspoonful vanilla extract
- half teaspoonful ground cinnamon
- one-fourth teaspoonful ground nutmeg
- half cupful raisins (optional)

Instructions:

1. In the Crockpot, combine rice, whole milk, granulated sugar, vanilla extract, ground cinnamon, and ground nutmeg.

2. Stir in raisins (if using).

3. Cover and cook on low for two-three hours, or until the rice is tender and the pudding is creamy.

4. Serve warm or chilled.

Duration for this recipe: two-three hours on low
Nutrients (per portion): Caloric content: 300, Amino content: 6g, Carb content: 55g, Fatty acid: 5g

5. CROCKPOT PEACH COBBLER

Servings: 2-4

Ingredients:

- four cupful canned or fresh peaches, sliced
- one cupful all-purpose flour
- one cupful granulated sugar
- one teaspoonful baking powder
- half teaspoonful salt
- half cupful milk
- one-fourth cupful unsalted butter, melted
- one teaspoonful vanilla extract
- half teaspoonful ground cinnamon

Instructions:

1. In the Crockpot, place sliced peaches.

2. In a bowl, whisk together flour, half cupful granulated sugar, baking powder, and salt.

3. Stir in milk, melted butter, and vanilla extract until smooth.

4. Pour the batter over the peaches in the Crockpot.

5. In a separate bowl, combine the remaining half cupful granulated sugar and ground cinnamon. Sprinkle this mixture over the batter.

6. Cover and cook on low for three-four hours, until the cobbler is set and the top is golden brown.

7. Serve warm with a scoop of vanilla ice cream.

Duration for this recipe: three-four hours on low

Nutrients (per portion, excluding ice cream):

- Caloric content: 280
- Amino content: 3g
- Carb content: 60g
- Fatty acid: 5g

6. CROCKPOT CHOCOLATE FONDUE

Servings: 3-4

Ingredients:

- one cupful heavy cream
- Twelve oz semisweet chocolate chips
- one teaspoonful vanilla extract
- Dippers (e.g., strawberries, banana slices, marshmallows, pretzels)

Instructions:

1. In the Crockpot, heat the heavy cream until hot but not boiling.

2. Stir in chocolate chips until fully melted and smooth.

3. Stir in vanilla extract.

4. Serve the chocolate fondue with dippers of your choice.

5. Keep the Crockpot on warm to maintain the fondue's consistency.

Duration for this recipe: Approximately 30 minutes

Nutrients (per portion, excluding dippers):

- Caloric content: 250, Amino content: 2g, Carb content: 20g, Fatty acid: 18g

7. CROCKPOT BANANAS FOSTER

Servings: 2-3

Ingredients:

- four ripe bananas, sliced
- half cupful unsalted butter
- one cupful brown sugar
- half teaspoonful ground cinnamon
- one-fourth cupful dark rum
- Vanilla ice cream (for serving)

Instructions:

1. In the Crockpot, combine banana slices.

2. In a saucepan, melt butter over medium heat. Stir in brown sugar and ground cinnamon.

3. Pour the butter-sugar mixture over the bananas in the Crockpot.

4. Cover and cook on low for one-two hours, until the bananas are soft and the sauce is bubbling.

5. Pour in the dark rum and carefully ignite it with a long lighter. Allow the flames to die down.

6. Serve the bananas foster over vanilla ice cream.

Duration for this recipe: one-two hours on low

Nutrients (per portion, excluding ice cream):

- Caloric content: 300
- Amino content: 1g
- Carb content: 45g
- Fatty acid: 16g

8. CROCKPOT LEMON BLUEBERRY BREAD PUDDING

Servings: 2-3

Ingredients:

- six cupful stale bread cubes (French or brioche bread works well)
- one cupful fresh or frozen blueberries
- half cupful granulated sugar
- one teaspoonful lemon zest
- one-fourth cupful lemon juice
- two cupful whole milk
- four eggs
- one-fourth cupful unsalted butter, melted
- one teaspoonful vanilla extract
- Powdered sugar (for dusting)

Instructions:

1. In the Crockpot, combine bread cubes and blueberries.
2. In a bowl, whisk together granulated sugar, lemon zest, lemon juice, whole milk, eggs, melted butter, and vanilla extract.
3. Pour the mixture over the bread and blueberries in the Crockpot.
4. Cover and cook on low for three-four hours, until the pudding is set.
5. Dust with powdered sugar before serving.

Duration for this recipe: three-four hours on low

Nutrients (per portion):

- Caloric content: 280, Amino content: 7g, Carb content: 40g, Fatty acid: 10g

9. CROCKPOT CHERRY DUMP CAKE

Servings: 3-4

Ingredients:

- two cans (2one oz each) cherry pie filling
- one box (15.Twnety five oz) yellow cake mix
- half cupful unsalted butter, melted
- half cupful chopped pecans (optional)
- Whipped cream (for serving)

Instructions:

1. In the Crockpot, spread cherry pie filling.
2. Sprinkle the dry cake mix evenly over the cherry filling.
3. Drizzle the melted butter over the cake mix.
4. If using pecans, sprinkle them over the butter.
5. Cover and cook on low for two-three hours, until the cake is set.
6. Serve with a dollop of whipped cream.

Duration for this recipe: two-three hours on low

Nutrients (per portion, excluding whipped cream):

- Caloric content: 320, Amino content: 2g, Carb content: 55g, Fatty acid: 12g

10. CROCKPOT TAPIOCA PUDDING

Servings: 2-3

Ingredients:

- half cupful small pearl tapioca
- three cupful whole milk
- half cupful granulated sugar
- two eggs, beaten
- one-fourth teaspoonful salt
- one teaspoonful vanilla extract
- Ground cinnamon (for garnish)

Instructions:

1. In a bowl, soak tapioca in two cupful of milk for 30 minutes.
2. Transfer the tapioca-milk mixture to the Crockpot.
3. Add the remaining one cupful of milk, granulated sugar, beaten eggs, and salt. Stir to combine.
4. Cover and cook on low for two-three hours, until the tapioca pearls are soft and the pudding is thickened.
5. Stir in vanilla extract.
6. Serve warm or chilled, garnished with ground cinnamon.

Duration for this recipe: two-three hours on low

Nutrients (per portion): Caloric content: 180, Amino content: 4g, Carb content: 32g, Fatty acid: 4g

CHAPTER 13:
SNACKS

1. CROCKPOT SPICY BUFFALO CHICKEN DIP

Servings: 2-3

Ingredients:

- two cupful cooked chicken, shredded
- eight oz cream cheese, softened
- one cupful shredded cheddar cheese
- half cupful blue cheese dressing
- half cupful hot sauce (adjust to taste)
- one-fourth cupful chopped green onions
- one-fourth cupful chopped celery
- Tortilla chips or vegetable sticks (for serving)

Instructions:

1. In the Crockpot, combine shredded chicken, softened cream cheese, shredded cheddar cheese, blue cheese dressing, hot sauce, and half of the chopped green onions.

2. Stir to combine all ingredients.

3. Cover and cook on low for one-two hours, until the dip is hot and bubbly.

4. Serve with tortilla chips or vegetable sticks.

5. Garnish with the remaining green onions and chopped celery.

Duration for this recipe: one-two hours on low

Nutrients (per portion, excluding chips or vegetable sticks):

- Caloric content: 200
- Amino content: 12g
- Carb content: 3g
- Fatty acid: 16g

2. CROCKPOT SPINACH AND ARTICHOKE DIP

Servings: 2-4

Ingredients:

- one cupful frozen chopped spinach, thawed and drained
- one can (fourteen oz) artichoke hearts, drained and chopped
- eight oz cream cheese, softened
- half cupful sour cream
- half cupful mayonnaise
- one cupful grated Parmesan cheese
- one cupful shredded mozzarella cheese
- two cloves garlic, minced
- half teaspoonful crushed red pepper flakes (optional)
- Tortilla chips or bread slices (for serving)

Instructions:

1. In the Crockpot, combine chopped spinach, chopped artichoke hearts, softened cream cheese, sour cream, mayonnaise, grated Parmesan cheese, shredded mozzarella cheese, minced garlic, and crushed red pepper flakes (if using).
2. Stir to combine all ingredients.
3. Cover and cook on low for one-two hours, until the dip is hot and bubbly.
4. Serve with tortilla chips or bread slices.

Duration for this recipe: one-two hours on low

Nutrients (per portion, excluding chips or bread):

- Caloric content: 250
- Amino content: 8g
- Carb content: 4g
- Fatty acid: 22g

3. CROCKPOT HONEY ROASTED NUTS

Servings: 3-5

Ingredients:

- four cupful mixed nuts (e.g., almonds, cashews, walnuts)
- one-fourth cupful honey
- two tablespoonful unsalted butter, melted
- one teaspoonful cinnamon
- half teaspoonful salt
- one-fourth teaspoonful cayenne pepper (adjust to taste)

Instructions:

1. In the Crockpot, combine mixed nuts.
2. In a bowl, whisk together honey, melted butter, cinnamon, salt, and cayenne pepper.
3. Pour the honey mixture over the nuts and stir to coat evenly.
4. Cover and cook on low for one-two hours, stirring every 30 minutes.
5. Spread the nuts on a baking sheet to cool.
6. Serve as a sweet and spicy snack.

Duration for this recipe: one-two hours on low

Nutrients (per portion):

- Caloric content: 200
- Amino content: 6g
- Carb content: 14g
- Fatty acid: 15g

4. CROCKPOT CINNAMON ALMONDS

Servings: 2-3

Ingredients:

- two cupful whole almonds
- half cupful granulated sugar
- one-fourth cupful brown sugar
- one tablespoonful ground cinnamon
- one-fourth teaspoonful salt
- one-fourth cupful water
- one teaspoonful vanilla extract

Instructions:

1. In the Crockpot, combine whole almonds.
2. In a bowl, whisk together granulated sugar, brown sugar, ground cinnamon, and salt.
3. Pour the sugar mixture over the almonds and toss to coat.
4. In a separate bowl, mix water and vanilla extract.
5. Pour the water mixture over the almonds and sugar.
6. Stir to combine.
7. Cover and cook on low for two-three hours, stirring every 30 minutes, until the almonds are coated and the sugar has crystallized.

8. Spread the almonds on a baking sheet to cool.

9. Serve as a sweet and crunchy snack.

Duration for this recipe: two-three hours on low

Nutrients (per portion):

- Caloric content: 180
- Amino content: 4g
- Carb content: 20g
- Fatty acid: 11g

5. CROCKPOT SWEET AND SAVORY MEATBALLS

Servings: 2-3

Ingredients:

- one lb frozen meatballs
- one cupful barbecue sauce
- half cupful grape jelly
- Toothpicks (for serving)

Instructions:

1. In the Crockpot, combine frozen meatballs, barbecue sauce, and grape jelly.

2. Stir to coat the meatballs evenly.

3. Cover and cook on low for two-three hours, until the meatballs are heated through and the sauce is thickened.

4. Serve with toothpicks for a sweet and savory snack.

Duration for this recipe: two-three hours on low

Nutrients (per portion):

- Caloric content: 160
- Amino content: 6g
- Carb content: 20g
- Fatty acid: 6g

6. CROCKPOT RANCH OYSTER CRACKERS

Servings: 2-4

Ingredients:

- one lb oyster crackers
- half cupful vegetable oil
- one packet ranch dressing mix
- half teaspoonful garlic powder
- half teaspoonful onion powder
- half teaspoonful dried dill

Instructions:

1. In the Crockpot, place oyster crackers.

2. In a bowl, mix vegetable oil, ranch dressing mix, garlic powder, onion powder, and dried dill.

3. Pour the mixture over the oyster crackers and toss to coat evenly.

4. Cover and cook on low for one-two hours, stirring every 30 minutes.

5. Allow the crackers to cool before serving as a flavorful snack.

Duration for this recipe: one-two hours on low

Nutrients (per portion):

- Caloric content: 120
- Amino content: 2g
- Carb content: 16g
- Fatty acid: 6g

7. CROCKPOT CARAMELIZED ONION DIP

Servings: 2-3

- three large onions, thinly sliced
- two tablespoonful unsalted butter
- one-fourth cupful mayonnaise
- one-fourth cupful sour cream
- half cupful cream cheese, softened
- one-fourth cupful grated Parmesan cheese
- one-fourth cupful shredded mozzarella cheese
- half teaspoonful salt
- one-fourth teaspoonful black pepper
- Potato chips or crackers (for serving)

Instructions:

1. In a skillet, melt unsalted butter over medium heat. Add thinly sliced onions and cook, stirring occasionally, until caramelized (about 20-30 minutes).

2. In the Crockpot, combine caramelized onions, mayonnaise, sour cream, softened cream cheese, grated Parmesan cheese, shredded mozzarella cheese, salt, and black pepper.

3. Stir to combine all ingredients.

4. Cover and cook on low for one-two hours, until the dip is hot and bubbly.

5. Serve with potato chips or crackers.

Duration for this recipe: one-two hours on low
Nutrients (per portion, excluding chips or crackers):

- Caloric content: 180, Amino content: 4g, Carb content: 6g, Fatty acid: 15g

8. CROCKPOT BBQ MEATBALL SLIDERS

Servings: 4-5

Ingredients:

- one lb frozen meatballs
- one cupful barbecue sauce
- half cupful shredded cheddar cheese
- Slider rolls
- Pickles (optional, for serving)

Instructions:

1. In the Crockpot, combine frozen meatballs and barbecue sauce.
2. Stir to coat the meatballs evenly.
3. Cover and cook on low for two-three hours, until the meatballs are heated through.
4. To assemble sliders, place a few meatballs on slider rolls, top with shredded cheddar cheese, and add pickles if desired.
5. Serve as a savory snack.

Duration for this recipe: two-three hours on low
Nutrients (per slider, excluding pickles):

- Caloric content: 250
- Amino content: 10g
- Carb content: 22g
- Fatty acid: 14g

9. CROCKPOT QUESO DIP

Servings: 1-2

Ingredients:

- two cupful shredded cheddar cheese
- one cupful shredded Monterey Jack cheese
- one can (ten oz) diced tomatoes with green chilies, undrained
- half cupful milk
- half cupful sour cream
- half teaspoonful ground cumin
- half teaspoonful chili powder
- Tortilla chips (for dipping)

Instructions:

1. In the Crockpot, combine shredded cheddar cheese, shredded Monterey Jack cheese, diced tomatoes with green chilies, milk, sour cream, ground cumin, and chili powder.
2. Stir to combine all ingredients.
3. Cover and cook on low for one-two hours, until the dip is hot and melted.
4. Serve with tortilla chips for a cheesy snack.

Duration for this recipe: one-two hours on low
Nutrients (per portion, excluding chips):

- Caloric content: 180, Amino content: 9g, Carb content: 5g, Fatty acid: 14g

10. CROCKPOT PIZZA DIP

Servings: 2-3

- eight oz cream cheese, softened
- one cupful shredded mozzarella cheese
- half cupful grated Parmesan cheese
- one cupful pizza sauce
- half cupful diced bell peppers
- half cupful sliced black olives
- half cupful sliced pepperoni
- half teaspoonful dried oregano
- Tortilla chips or baguette slices (for dipping)

Instructions:

1. In the Crockpot, combine softened cream cheese, shredded mozzarella cheese, grated Parmesan cheese, pizza sauce, diced bell peppers, sliced black olives, and sliced pepperoni.
2. Stir to combine all ingredients.
3. Sprinkle dried oregano on top.
4. Cover and cook on low for one-two hours, until the dip is hot and bubbly.
5. Serve with tortilla chips or baguette slices for a pizza-inspired snack.

Duration for this recipe: one-two hours on low
Nutrients (per portion, excluding chips or bread):

- Caloric content: 200, Amino content: 9g, Carb content: 4g, Fatty acid: 16g

CHAPTER 14:
STAPLE AND SAUCES

1. CROCKPOT TOMATO SAUCE

Servings: 2-3
Ingredients:
- two cans (2eight oz each) crushed tomatoes
- one onion, finely chopped
- four cloves garlic, minced
- two teaspoonful dried basil
- one teaspoonful dried oregano
- one teaspoonful sugar
- Salt and black pepper to taste
- two tablespoonful olive oil

Instructions:
1. In the Crockpot, combine crushed tomatoes, chopped onion, minced garlic, dried basil, dried oregano, sugar, salt, black pepper, and olive oil.
2. Stir to combine all ingredients.

3. Cover and cook on low for six-eight hours, allowing the flavors to meld.
4. Use this sauce for pasta, pizza, or as a base for various dishes.
   Duration for this recipe: six-eight hours on low
   Nutrients (per portion, approx. half cupful):
- Caloric content: 50
- Amino content: 2g
- Carb content: 10g
- Fatty acid: 2g

2. CROCKPOT BEEF BROTH

Servings: 1-2
Ingredients:
- two lbs beef bones
- one onion, chopped
- two carrots, chopped
- two celery stalks, chopped

- four cloves garlic, smashed
- two bay leaves
- one teaspoonful black peppercorns
- Water to cover

Instructions:

1. In the Crockpot, combine beef bones, chopped onion, chopped carrots, chopped celery, smashed garlic, bay leaves, and black peppercorns.

2. Add enough water to cover the ingredients.

3. Cover and cook on low for eight-ten hours to make a rich beef broth.

4. Strain the broth and use it in soups, stews, and other recipes.

Duration for this recipe: eight-ten hours on low
Nutrients (per one-cupful serving):

- Caloric content: 10
- Amino content: 1g
- Carb content: 2g
- Fatty acid: 0g

3. CROCKPOT MARINARA SAUCE

Servings: 2-3
Ingredients:

- two cans (2eight oz each) crushed tomatoes
- one onion, finely chopped
- four cloves garlic, minced
- two teaspoonful dried basil
- one teaspoonful dried oregano
- one teaspoonful sugar
- Salt and black pepper to taste
- two tablespoonful olive oil

Instructions:

1. In the Crockpot, combine crushed tomatoes, chopped onion, minced garlic, dried basil, dried oregano, sugar, salt, black pepper, and olive oil.

2. Stir to combine all ingredients.

3. Cover and cook on low for six-eight hours, allowing the flavors to meld.

4. Use this sauce for pasta, pizza, or as a base for various dishes.

Duration for this recipe: six-eight hours on low
Nutrients (per portion, approx. half cupful):

- Caloric content: 50

- Amino content: 2g
- Carb content: 10g
- Fatty acid: 2g

4. CROCKPOT VEGETABLE BROTH

Servings: 2-4
Ingredients:

- four cupful mixed vegetable scraps (e.g., carrot peels, onion skins, celery ends)
- one onion, chopped
- two carrots, chopped
- two celery stalks, chopped
- four cloves garlic, smashed
- two bay leaves
- one teaspoonful black peppercorns
- Water to cover

Instructions:

1. In the Crockpot, combine mixed vegetable scraps, chopped onion, chopped carrots, chopped celery, smashed garlic, bay leaves, and black peppercorns.

2. Add enough water to cover the ingredients.

3. Cover and cook on low for six-eight hours to make a flavorful vegetable broth.

4. Strain the broth and use it in soups, stews, and other recipes.

Duration for this recipe: six-eight hours on low
Nutrients (per one-cupful serving):

- Caloric content: 5
- Amino content: 0g
- Carb content: 1g
- Fatty acid: 0g

5. CROCKPOT ALFREDO SAUCE

Servings: 3-5

- one cupful heavy cream
- half cupful unsalted butter
- one half cupful grated Parmesan cheese
- two cloves garlic, minced
- one teaspoonful salt
- half teaspoonful black pepper
- half teaspoonful nutmeg (optional)
- one-fourth cupful chopped fresh parsley (for garnish)

- Cooked fettuccine or pasta of your choice

Instructions:

1.   In the Crockpot, combine heavy cream, unsalted butter, grated Parmesan cheese, minced garlic, salt, black pepper, and nutmeg (if using).

2.   Stir to combine all ingredients.

3.   Cover and cook on low for two-three hours, stirring occasionally, until the sauce is creamy and well-blended.

4.   Serve the Alfredo sauce over cooked fettuccine or your preferred pasta.

5.   Garnish with chopped fresh parsley.

Duration for this recipe: two-three hours on low
Nutrients (per portion, excluding pasta):

- Caloric content: 300
- Amino content: 8g
- Carb content: 2g
- Fatty acid: 29g

6. CROCKPOT CHICKEN STOCK

Servings: 2-3

Ingredients:

- two lbs chicken bones or carcass
- one onion, chopped
- two carrots, chopped
- two celery stalks, chopped
- four cloves garlic, smashed
- two bay leaves
- one teaspoonful black peppercorns
- Water to cover

Instructions:

1.   In the Crockpot, combine chicken bones or carcass, chopped onion, chopped carrots, chopped celery, smashed garlic, bay leaves, and black peppercorns.

2.   Add enough water to cover the ingredients.

3.   Cover and cook on low for eight-ten hours to create a flavorful chicken stock.

4.   Strain the stock and use it as a base for soups and sauces.

Duration for this recipe: eight-ten hours on low
Nutrients (per one-cupful serving):

- Caloric content: 10
- Amino content: 1g

- Carb content: 1g
- Fatty acid: 0g

7. CROCKPOT BBQ SAUCE

Servings: 1-2

- two cupful ketchup
- half cupful brown sugar
- one-fourth cupful apple cider vinegar
- two tablespoonful Worcestershire sauce
- one teaspoonful smoked paprika
- one teaspoonful garlic powder
- half teaspoonful onion powder
- half teaspoonful black pepper
- half teaspoonful salt
- one-fourth teaspoonful cayenne pepper (adjust to taste)

Instructions:

1.   In the Crockpot, combine ketchup, brown sugar, apple cider vinegar, Worcestershire sauce, smoked paprika, garlic powder, onion powder, black pepper, salt, and cayenne pepper.

2.   Stir to combine all ingredients.

3.   Cover and cook on low for two-three hours, allowing the flavors to meld.

4.   Use this BBQ sauce for grilling, marinating, or dipping.

Duration for this recipe: two-three hours on low
Nutrients (per portion, approx. two tablespoonful):

- Caloric content: 50
- Amino content: 0g
- Carb content: 13g
- Fatty acid: 0g

8. CROCKPOT CHILI SAUCE

Servings: 2-3

Ingredients:

- three cupful chopped tomatoes
- one cupful chopped red bell pepper
- half cupful chopped onion
- one-fourth cupful apple cider vinegar
- one-fourth cupful brown sugar
- one teaspoonful salt
- half teaspoonful red pepper flakes

- half teaspoonful black pepper
- half teaspoonful paprika

Instructions:

1. In the Crockpot, combine chopped tomatoes, chopped red bell pepper, chopped onion, apple cider vinegar, brown sugar, salt, red pepper flakes, black pepper, and paprika.

2. Stir to combine all ingredients.

3. Cover and cook on low for four-six hours, until the sauce thickens and the flavors meld.

4. Use this chili sauce for condiments or as a dipping sauce.

Duration for this recipe: four-six hours on low

Nutrients (per portion, approx. two tablespoonful):

- Caloric content: 40
- Amino content: 1g
- Carb content: 10g
- Fatty acid: 0g

9. CROCKPOT PESTO SAUCE

Servings: 4-6

Ingredients:

- two cupful fresh basil leaves
- half cupful grated Parmesan cheese
- one-fourth cupful pine nuts
- two cloves garlic
- half cupful olive oil
- half teaspoonful salt
- one-fourth teaspoonful black pepper
- one-fourth cupful grated Pecorino Romano cheese

Instructions:

1. In a food processor, combine fresh basil leaves, grated Parmesan cheese, pine nuts, and garlic.

2. Pulse until well combined.

3. Transfer the mixture to the Crockpot.

4. Stir in olive oil, salt, black pepper, and grated Pecorino Romano cheese.

5. Cover and cook on low for two-three hours, allowing the flavors to meld.

6. Use this pesto sauce for pasta, sandwiches, or as a dip.

Duration for this recipe: two-three hours on low

Nutrients (per portion, approx. two tablespoonful):

- Caloric content: 100
- Amino content: 2g
- Carb content: 2g
- Fatty acid: 10g

10. CROCKPOT ENCHILADA SAUCE

Servings: 2-3

Ingredients:

- two cans (fourteen oz each) crushed tomatoes
- one-fourth cupful chili powder
- two teaspoonful ground cumin
- one teaspoonful onion powder
- one teaspoonful garlic powder
- half teaspoonful oregano
- half teaspoonful salt
- one-fourth teaspoonful black pepper
- one-fourth teaspoonful cayenne pepper (adjust to taste)
- two cupful chicken or vegetable broth

Instructions:

1. In the Crockpot, combine crushed tomatoes, chili powder, ground cumin, onion powder, garlic powder, oregano, salt, black pepper, and cayenne pepper.

2. Stir to combine all ingredients.

3. Add chicken or vegetable broth and mix well.

4. Cover and cook on low for four-six hours, allowing the flavors to meld.

5. Use this enchilada sauce for making enchiladas, as a topping, or as a marinade.

Duration for this recipe: four-six hours on low

Nutrients (per portion, approx. one-fourth cupful):

- Caloric content: 25
- Amino content: 1g
- Carb content: 5g
- Fatty acid: 0g

CHAPTER 15: VEGETARIAN

1. CROCKPOT VEGETARIAN CHILI

Servings: 1-2

Ingredients:
- two cans (fourteen oz each) diced tomatoes
- one can (fifteen oz) black beans, drained and rinsed
- one can (fifteen oz) kidney beans, drained and rinsed
- one can (fifteen oz) pinto beans, drained and rinsed
- two cupful vegetable broth
- one onion, chopped
- one red bell pepper, chopped
- one green bell pepper, chopped
- two cloves garlic, minced
- two tablespoonful chili powder
- one teaspoonful ground cumin
- one teaspoonful paprika
- half teaspoonful cayenne pepper (adjust to taste)
- Salt and black pepper to taste
- one cupful frozen corn kernels

Instructions:
1. In the Crockpot, combine diced tomatoes, black beans, kidney beans, pinto beans, vegetable broth, chopped onion, chopped red bell pepper, chopped green bell pepper, minced garlic, chili powder, ground cumin, paprika, cayenne pepper, salt, and black pepper.
2. Stir to combine all ingredients.
3. Cover and cook on low for six-eight hours.
4. Add frozen corn kernels in the last hour of cooking.

5. Serve the chili with your favorite toppings, such as shredded cheese, sour cream, and chopped cilantro.

Duration for this recipe: six-eight hours on low
Nutrients (per portion, approximately one cupful):
- Caloric content: 250
- Amino content: 10g
- Carb content: 47g
- Fatty acid: 2g

2. CROCKPOT VEGETARIAN LASAGNA

Servings: 2-3
Ingredients:
- nine lasagna noodles, uncooked
- two cans (fourteen oz each) diced tomatoes
- two cupful tomato sauce
- two cupful ricotta cheese
- two cupful shredded mozzarella cheese
- half cupful grated Parmesan cheese
- one egg
- one teaspoonful dried basil
- one teaspoonful dried oregano
- Salt and black pepper to taste
- two cupful fresh spinach
- one cupful sliced mushrooms
- one cupful chopped zucchini

Instructions:
1. In a bowl, combine ricotta cheese, one cupful of shredded mozzarella cheese, grated Parmesan cheese, egg, dried basil, dried oregano, salt, and black pepper.
2. In the Crockpot, layer with one can of diced tomatoes, followed by three lasagna noodles (break as needed to fit), half of the cheese mixture, half of the fresh spinach, half of the sliced mushrooms, half of the chopped zucchini, and half of the second can of diced tomatoes.
3. Repeat the layers.
4. Top with the remaining shredded mozzarella cheese.
5. Cover and cook on low for four-five hours.
6. Let it rest for 1five-30 minutes before serving.

Duration for this recipe: four-five hours on low
Nutrients (per portion, approximately 1/six of the lasagna):
- Caloric content: 400
- Amino content: 23g
- Carb content: 35g
- Fatty acid: 18g

3. CROCKPOT VEGETABLE CURRY

Servings: 2-4
Ingredients:
- two cupful chopped potatoes
- two cupful cauliflower florets
- one cupful chopped carrots
- one cupful chopped bell peppers
- one cupful chopped onion
- two cloves garlic, minced
- one can (fourteen oz) diced tomatoes
- one can (fourteen oz) chickpeas, drained and rinsed
- one can (fourteen oz) coconut milk
- two tablespoonful curry powder
- one teaspoonful ground cumin
- one teaspoonful ground coriander
- half teaspoonful turmeric
- Salt and black pepper to taste
- Fresh cilantro (for garnish)
- Cooked rice (for serving)

Instructions:
1. In the Crockpot, combine chopped potatoes, cauliflower florets, chopped carrots, chopped bell peppers, chopped onion, minced garlic, diced tomatoes, chickpeas, and coconut milk.
2. Stir in curry powder, ground cumin, ground coriander, turmeric, salt, and black pepper.
3. Cover and cook on low for six-eight hours.
4. Serve the vegetable curry over cooked rice and garnish with fresh cilantro.

Duration for this recipe: six-eight hours on low
Nutrients (per portion, excluding rice):
- Caloric content: 250
- Amino content: 7g
- Carb content: 25g
- Fatty acid: 14g

4. CROCKPOT BUTTERNUT SQUASH SOUP

Servings: 3-5

- four cupful butternut squash, peeled and diced
- one apple, peeled and chopped
- one onion, chopped
- two cloves garlic, minced
- four cupful vegetable broth
- one teaspoonful dried thyme
- half teaspoonful ground cinnamon
- Salt and black pepper to taste
- half cupful heavy cream (optional)
- Chopped fresh chives (for garnish)

Instructions:

1.   In the Crockpot, combine diced butternut squash, chopped apple, chopped onion, minced garlic, vegetable broth, dried thyme, ground cinnamon, salt, and black pepper.

2.   Cover and cook on low for six-eight hours.

3.   Use an immersion blender to puree the soup until smooth.

4.   If desired, stir in heavy cream for added richness.

5.   Garnish with chopped fresh chives.

Duration for this recipe: six-eight hours on low
Nutrients (per portion, approximately one cupful without heavy cream):

- Caloric content: 80
- Amino content: 2g
- Carb content: 20g
- Fatty acid: 0g

5. CROCKPOT MUSHROOM STROGANOFF

Servings: 2-3
Ingredients:

- 1six oz mushrooms, sliced
- one onion, chopped
- two cloves garlic, minced
- two cans (10.five oz each) cream of mushroom soup
- one cupful vegetable broth
- one tablespoonful Worcestershire sauce
- one teaspoonful paprika
- Salt and black pepper to taste
- one cupful sour cream
- Cooked egg noodles (for serving)

Instructions:

1.   In the Crockpot, combine sliced mushrooms, chopped onion, minced garlic, cream of mushroom soup, vegetable broth, Worcestershire sauce, paprika, salt, and black pepper.

2.   Cover and cook on low for six-eight hours.

3.   Stir in sour cream.

4.   Serve the mushroom stroganoff over cooked egg noodles.

Duration for this recipe: six-eight hours on low
Nutrients (per portion, excluding noodles):

- Caloric content: 200
- Amino content: 4g
- Carb content: 8g
- Fatty acid: 16g

6. CROCKPOT RATATOUILLE

Servings: 2-3
Ingredients:

- two medium eggplants, diced
- two zucchinis, diced
- two bell peppers, diced
- two onions, chopped
- four cloves garlic, minced
- two cans (fourteen oz each) diced tomatoes
- two teaspoonful dried thyme
- one teaspoonful dried oregano
- Salt and black pepper to taste
- one-fourth cupful chopped fresh basil
- one-fourth cupful chopped fresh parsley

Instructions:

1.   In the Crockpot, combine diced eggplants, diced zucchinis, diced bell peppers, chopped onions, minced garlic, diced tomatoes, dried thyme, dried oregano, salt, and black pepper.

2.   Stir to combine all ingredients.

3.   Cover and cook on low for six-eight hours.

4.   Stir in fresh basil and fresh parsley before serving.

Duration for this recipe: six-eight hours on low

Nutrients (per portion, approximately one cupful):

- Caloric content: 60
- Amino content: 2g
- Carb content: 15g
- Fatty acid: 0g

7. CROCKPOT POTATO LEEK SOUP

Servings: 2-3

Ingredients:

- four cupful sliced leeks (white and light green parts)
- four cupful diced potatoes
- one onion, chopped
- four cupful vegetable broth
- two cloves garlic, minced
- one teaspoonful dried thyme
- Salt and black pepper to taste
- one cupful heavy cream
- Chopped fresh chives (for garnish)

Instructions:

1. In the Crockpot, combine sliced leeks, diced potatoes, chopped onion, vegetable broth, minced garlic, dried thyme, salt, and black pepper.
2. Cover and cook on low for six-eight hours.
3. Use an immersion blender to puree the soup until smooth.
4. Stir in heavy cream for a creamy texture.
5. Garnish with chopped fresh chives.

Duration for this recipe: six-eight hours on low

Nutrients (per portion, approximately one cupful):

- Caloric content: 150
- Amino content: 2g
- Carb content: 20g
- Fatty acid: 7g

8. CROCKPOT LENTIL SOUP

Servings: 1-2

Ingredients:

- two cupful green or brown lentils
- one onion, chopped
- two carrots, chopped
- two celery stalks, chopped
- two cloves garlic, minced
- one can (fourteen oz) diced tomatoes
- six cupful vegetable broth
- one teaspoonful ground cumin
- one teaspoonful ground coriander
- half teaspoonful smoked paprika
- Salt and black pepper to taste
- Fresh lemon juice (for serving)
- Chopped fresh cilantro (for garnish)

Instructions:

1. In the Crockpot, combine lentils, chopped onion, chopped carrots, chopped celery, minced garlic, diced tomatoes, vegetable broth, ground cumin, ground coriander, smoked paprika, salt, and black pepper.
2. Stir to combine all ingredients.
3. Cover and cook on low for six-eight hours.
4. Add a squeeze of fresh lemon juice before serving and garnish with chopped fresh cilantro.

Duration for this recipe: six-eight hours on low

Nutrients (per portion, approximately one cupful):

- Caloric content: 150
- Amino content: 10g
- Carb content: 25g
- Fatty acid: 1g

9. CROCKPOT QUINOA AND VEGETABLE STEW

Servings: 2-3

- one cupful quinoa, rinsed
- four cupful vegetable broth
- two carrots, chopped
- two celery stalks, chopped
- one bell pepper, chopped
- one zucchini, chopped
- one can (fourteen oz) diced tomatoes
- two cloves garlic, minced
- one teaspoonful dried thyme
- one teaspoonful smoked paprika
- Salt and black pepper to taste
- one cupful fresh spinach

Instructions:

1. In the Crockpot, combine quinoa, vegetable broth, chopped carrots, chopped celery, chopped bell pepper, chopped zucchini, diced tomatoes, minced garlic, dried thyme, smoked paprika, salt, and black pepper.

2. Stir to combine all ingredients.

3. Cover and cook on low for four-six hours.

4. Add fresh spinach in the last hour of cooking.

Duration for this recipe: four-six hours on low

Nutrients (per portion, approximately one cupful):

- Caloric content: 120
- Amino content: 5g
- Carb content: 23g
- Fatty acid: 1g

10. CROCKPOT VEGETABLE BIRYANI

Servings: 4-5

Ingredients:

- two cupful basmati rice, rinsed and drained
- four cupful mixed vegetables (e.g., peas, carrots, bell peppers)
- one onion, chopped
- two cloves garlic, minced
- two teaspoonful curry powder
- one teaspoonful ground cumin
- half teaspoonful ground turmeric
- half teaspoonful ground coriander
- one-fourth teaspoonful cayenne pepper (adjust to taste)
- four cupful vegetable broth
- Salt and black pepper to taste
- Chopped fresh cilantro (for garnish)
- Slivered almonds (for garnish)

Instructions:

1. In the Crockpot, combine basmati rice, mixed vegetables, chopped onion, minced garlic, curry powder, ground cumin, ground turmeric, ground coriander, cayenne pepper, vegetable broth, salt, and black pepper.

2. Stir to combine all ingredients.

3. Cover and cook on low for three-four hours until the rice is tender and the liquid is absorbed.

4. Garnish with chopped fresh cilantro and slivered almonds.

Duration for this recipe: three-four hours on low

Nutrients (per portion, approximately one cupful):

- Caloric content: 200
- Amino content: 5g
- Carb content: 40g
- Fatty acid: 1g

CHAPTER 16:
SOUPS AND STEW

1. CROCKPOT CHICKEN NOODLE SOUP

Servings: 1-2

Ingredients:

- four boneless, skinless chicken breasts
- eight cupful chicken broth
- three carrots, sliced
- three celery stalks, sliced
- one onion, chopped
- three cloves garlic, minced
- two teaspoonful dried thyme
- two teaspoonful dried rosemary
- one bay leaf
- two cupful egg noodles
- Salt and black pepper to taste
- Fresh parsley (for garnish)

Instructions:

1. In the Crockpot, place chicken breasts, chicken broth, carrots, celery, onion, minced garlic, dried thyme, dried rosemary, and bay leaf.
2. Cover and cook on low for six-eight hours.
3. Shred the cooked chicken and return it to the Crockpot.
4. Add egg noodles and cook on low for an additional 30 minutes or until the noodles are tender.
5. Season with salt and black pepper.
6. Garnish with fresh parsley before serving.

Duration for this recipe: six-eight hours + 30 minutes on low

Nutrients (per portion, approximately one cupful):

- Caloric content: 150
- Amino content: 15g
- Carb content: 15g

- Fatty acid: 3g

2. CROCKPOT GREEN BEEF STEW

Servings: 2-4
Ingredients:

- two lbs stewing beef, cubed
- four cupful beef broth
- four carrots, sliced
- four potatoes, diced
- two onions, chopped
- two cloves garlic, minced
- two teaspoonful dried thyme
- one teaspoonful dried rosemary
- one bay leaf
- Salt and black pepper to taste
- one cupful frozen peas
- Fresh parsley (for garnish)

Instructions:

1. In the Crockpot, combine cubed stewing beef, beef broth, sliced carrots, diced potatoes, chopped onions, minced garlic, dried thyme, dried rosemary, bay leaf, salt, and black pepper.
2. Cover and cook on low for six-eight hours.
3. Add frozen peas in the last hour of cooking.
4. Remove the bay leaf before serving.
5. Garnish with fresh parsley.

Duration for this recipe: six-eight hours on low
Nutrients (per portion, approximately one cupful):

- Caloric content: 200
- Amino content: 15g
- Carb content: 20g
- Fatty acid: 6g

3. CROCKPOT MINESTRONE SOUP

Servings: 2-3
Ingredients:

- two cans (fourteen oz each) diced tomatoes
- four cupful vegetable broth
- two carrots, sliced
- two celery stalks, sliced
- one onion, chopped
- three cloves garlic, minced
- one cupful small pasta (e.g., ditalini or small shells)
- one can (fifteen oz) kidney beans, drained and rinsed
- one can (fifteen oz) cannellini beans, drained and rinsed
- two teaspoonful dried basil
- one teaspoonful dried oregano
- Salt and black pepper to taste
- Fresh basil (for garnish)
- Grated Parmesan cheese (for garnish)

Instructions:

1. In the Crockpot, combine diced tomatoes, vegetable broth, sliced carrots, sliced celery, chopped onion, minced garlic, small pasta, kidney beans, cannellini beans, dried basil, dried oregano, salt, and black pepper.
2. Cover and cook on low for six-eight hours.
3. Garnish with fresh basil and grated Parmesan cheese before serving.

Duration for this recipe: six-eight hours on low
Nutrients (per portion, approximately one cupful):

- Caloric content: 150
- Amino content: 6g
- Carb content: 30g
- Fatty acid: 1g

4. CROCKPOT VEGETARIAN LENTIL STEW

Servings: 2-3
Ingredients:

- two cupful brown or green lentils
- eight cupful vegetable broth
- two carrots, chopped
- two celery stalks, chopped
- one onion, chopped
- two cloves garlic, minced
- two teaspoonful ground cumin
- one teaspoonful smoked paprika
- half teaspoonful ground coriander
- one-fourth teaspoonful cayenne pepper (adjust to taste)
- Salt and black pepper to taste

- two cupful fresh spinach
- Fresh lemon juice (for serving)

Instructions:

1.   In the Crockpot, combine brown or green lentils, vegetable broth, chopped carrots, chopped celery, chopped onion, minced garlic, ground cumin, smoked paprika, ground coriander, cayenne pepper, salt, and black pepper.

2.   Cover and cook on low for six-eight hours.

3.   Add fresh spinach in the last hour of cooking.

4.   Serve with a squeeze of fresh lemon juice.

Duration for this recipe: six-eight hours on low

Nutrients (per portion, approximately one cupful):

- Caloric content: 150
- Amino content: 10g
- Carb content: 25g
- Fatty acid: 1g

5. CROCKPOT CHICKEN AND RICE SOUP

Servings: 1-3

Ingredients:

- four boneless, skinless chicken breasts
- eight cupful chicken broth
- two carrots, sliced
- two celery stalks, sliced
- one onion, chopped
- three cloves garlic, minced
- two cupful long-grain rice
- two teaspoonful dried thyme
- two teaspoonful dried rosemary
- Salt and black pepper to taste
- Fresh parsley (for garnish)

Instructions:

1.   In the Crockpot, place chicken breasts, chicken broth, sliced carrots, sliced celery, chopped onion, minced garlic, dried thyme, dried rosemary, salt, and black pepper.

2.   Cover and cook on low for six-eight hours.

3.   Shred the cooked chicken and return it to the Crockpot.

4.   Add long-grain rice and cook on low for an additional 30 minutes or until the rice is tender.

5.   Garnish with fresh parsley before serving.

Duration for this recipe: six-eight hours + 30 minutes on low

Nutrients (per portion, approximately one cupful):

- Caloric content: 200
- Amino content: 15g
- Carb content: 30g
- Fatty acid: 2g

6. CROCKPOT POTATO SOUP

Servings: 2-3

Ingredients:

- six cupful diced potatoes
- two cupful diced leeks (white and light green parts)
- four cupful vegetable broth
- two cloves garlic, minced
- one teaspoonful dried thyme
- half teaspoonful dried rosemary
- Salt and black pepper to taste
- one cupful heavy cream
- Shredded cheddar cheese (for garnish)
- Crumbled bacon (for garnish)
- Sliced green onions (for garnish)

Instructions:

1.   In the Crockpot, combine diced potatoes, diced leeks, vegetable broth, minced garlic, dried thyme, dried rosemary, salt, and black pepper.

2.   Cover and cook on low for six-eight hours.

3.   Use an immersion blender to puree the soup until smooth.

4.   Stir in heavy cream.

5.   Garnish with shredded cheddar cheese, crumbled bacon, and sliced green onions.

Duration for this recipe: six-eight hours on low

Nutrients (per portion, approximately one cupful):

- Caloric content: 250
- Amino content: 4g
- Carb content: 30g
- Fatty acid: 12g

7. CROCKPOT SPLIT PEA SOUP

Servings: 2-5
Ingredients:

- two cupful dried split peas
- eight cupful vegetable broth
- two carrots, chopped
- two celery stalks, chopped
- one onion, chopped
- two cloves garlic, minced
- one teaspoonful dried thyme
- half teaspoonful dried rosemary
- Salt and black pepper to taste
- Smoked ham hock or smoked tofu (for flavor, optional)
- Fresh parsley (for garnish)

Instructions:

1. In the Crockpot, combine dried split peas, vegetable broth, chopped carrots, chopped celery, chopped onion, minced garlic, dried thyme, dried rosemary, salt, black pepper, and a smoked ham hock or smoked tofu for added flavor (optional).
2. Cover and cook on low for six-eight hours.
3. Remove the ham hock (if used) and shred the meat, then return it to the soup.
4. Garnish with fresh parsley before serving.

Duration for this recipe: six-eight hours on low
Nutrients (per portion, approximately one cupful, without ham hock):

- Caloric content: 150
- Amino content: 10g
- Carb content: 30g
- Fatty acid: 1g

8. CROCKPOT BEEF AND BARLEY STEW

Servings: 2-4
Ingredients:

- two lbs stewing beef, cubed
- eight cupful beef broth
- two carrots, sliced
- two celery stalks, sliced
- one onion, chopped
- two cloves garlic, minced
- one cupful pearl barley
- two teaspoonful dried thyme
- one teaspoonful dried rosemary
- Salt and black pepper to taste
- Fresh parsley (for garnish)

Instructions:

1. In the Crockpot, combine cubed stewing beef, beef broth, sliced carrots, sliced celery, chopped onion, minced garlic, pearl barley, dried thyme, dried rosemary, salt, and black pepper.
2. Cover and cook on low for six-eight hours.
3. Garnish with fresh parsley before serving.

Duration for this recipe: six-eight hours on low
Nutrients (per portion, approximately one cupful):

- Caloric content: 200
- Amino content: 15g
- Carb content: 20g
- Fatty acid: 6g

9. CROCKPOT TOMATO BASIL SOUP

Servings: 2-3
Ingredients:

- four cupful diced tomatoes
- four cupful vegetable broth
- two cloves garlic, minced
- one teaspoonful dried basil
- Salt and black pepper to taste
- one cupful heavy cream
- Fresh basil (for garnish)
- Grated Parmesan cheese (for garnish)

Instructions:

1. In the Crockpot, combine diced tomatoes, vegetable broth, minced garlic, dried basil, salt, and black pepper.
2. Cover and cook on low for six-eight hours.
3. Use an immersion blender to puree the soup until smooth.
4. Stir in heavy cream.
5. Garnish with fresh basil and grated Parmesan cheese.

Duration for this recipe: six-eight hours on low
Nutrients (per portion, approximately one cupful):

- Caloric content: 150

- Amino content: 2g
- Carb content: 15g
- Fatty acid: 9g

10. CROCKPOT BLACK BEAN SOUP

Servings: 2-3

Ingredients:

- two cans (fourteen oz each) black beans, drained and rinsed
- four cupful vegetable broth
- one onion, chopped
- two cloves garlic, minced
- two teaspoonful ground cumin
- one teaspoonful chili powder
- half teaspoonful paprika
- one-fourth teaspoonful cayenne pepper (adjust to taste)
- Salt and black pepper to taste
- half cupful sour cream
- Chopped fresh cilantro (for garnish)
- Sliced green onions (for garnish)

Instructions:

1. In the Crockpot, combine black beans, vegetable broth, chopped onion, minced garlic, ground cumin, chili powder, paprika, cayenne pepper, salt, and black pepper.

2. Cover and cook on low for six-eight hours.

3. Use an immersion blender to puree a portion of the soup for a thicker texture.

4. Stir in sour cream.

5. Garnish with chopped fresh cilantro and sliced green onions.

Duration for this recipe: six-eight hours on low

Nutrients (per portion, approximately one cupful):

- Caloric content: 120
- Amino content: 3g
- Carb content: 10g
- Fatty acid: 5g

CONCLUSION

As we reach the end of our culinary journey through "The Ultimate Crockpot Cookbook for Busy People," it's time to reflect on the remarkable adventure we've embarked on. We've explored the world of slow cooking, unraveling its secrets, and discovered how this unassuming kitchen appliance can transform your busy life into one filled with delectable flavors and effortless dining.

The Crockpot, with its gentle, time-tested methods, has allowed us to savor global cuisines, from comforting stews to exotic curries, without the stress of laborious cooking. We've dived into the art of layering ingredients, mastering the craft of slow-cooked perfection. Whether you're a beginner in the kitchen or a seasoned chef, this cookbook has empowered you to create restaurant-quality meals with minimal effort.

In our journey, we've explored the subtle distinctions between Crockpots and slow cookers, demystified the allure of the Instant Pot, and guided you in choosing the perfect appliance that suits your needs. You've equipped your kitchen with essential tools and accessories, ensuring a seamless and enjoyable cooking experience. You've learned to handle your Crockpot with care, extend its longevity, and prevent those pesky scratches that can mar its beauty.

We've combined the essence of traditional recipes with the convenience of Crockpot cooking, creating an amalgamation of flavors that are sure to tantalize your taste buds and inspire your culinary creativity.

With each recipe, you've not only nourished your body but also your soul. The joy of savoring a meal you've prepared with your own hands, the stories shared around the dining table, and the culinary adventures that await you are what make cooking a truly enriching experience.

As you continue your journey in the kitchen, remember that the Crockpot is not just an appliance but a culinary companion, a reliable friend that will always be there to help you create wonderful memories and nourish your loved ones.

We hope that "The Ultimate Crockpot Cookbook for Busy People" has inspired you to explore new tastes, broaden your culinary horizons, and embrace the convenience and deliciousness that Crockpot cooking has to offer. As you embark on your own culinary adventures, remember to have fun, savor the process, and savor every bite.

Thank you for joining us on this flavorful journey. May your Crockpot continue to be your partner in creating wonderful meals and lasting memories. Happy slow cooking!

Warm regards,

BONUS:
GLOBAL CUISINE

1. TERIYAKI TACOS

Ingredients:
- two lbs boneless chicken thighs
- half cupful teriyaki sauce
- one-fourth cupful soy sauce
- one-fourth cupful brown sugar
- two cloves garlic, minced
- one teaspoonful ginger, minced
- Flour tortillas
- Sliced green onions
- Sliced bell peppers

Instructions:

1. In the Crockpot, combine chicken thighs, teriyaki sauce, soy sauce, brown sugar, garlic, and ginger.

2. Cover and cook on low for four-six hours, or until the chicken is tender.

3. Shred the chicken and serve in flour tortillas with sliced green onions and bell peppers.

Duration for this recipe: four-six hours on low

Nutrients (per portion, without tortillas and toppings):
- Caloric content: 220
- Amino content: 24g
- Carb content: 9g
- Fatty acid: 9g

2. FUSION CHILI CON CARNE

Ingredients:
- one lb ground beef
- one onion, chopped
- two cloves garlic, minced
- two cans (fifteen oz each) kidney beans, drained and rinsed
- one can (2eight oz) diced tomatoes

- two tablespoonful chili powder
- one teaspoonful cumin
- Salt and black pepper to taste
- Shredded cheddar cheese (for garnish)

Instructions:

1. In a skillet, brown the ground beef and drain excess fat.

2. In the Crockpot, combine the browned beef, chopped onion, minced garlic, kidney beans, diced tomatoes, chili powder, cumin, salt, and black pepper.

3. Cover and cook on low for six-eight hours.

4. Serve with shredded cheddar cheese on top.

Duration for this recipe: six-eight hours on low
Nutrients (per portion, without cheese):
- Caloric content: 250
- Amino content: 20g
- Carb content: 25g
- Fatty acid: 8g

3. ASIAN BBQ FUSION CHICKEN

Ingredients:
- two lbs boneless chicken thighs
- half cupful barbecue sauce
- one-fourth cupful soy sauce
- two tablespoonful honey
- two cloves garlic, minced
- one teaspoonful ginger, minced
- Sliced green onions (for garnish)
- Sesame seeds (for garnish)

Instructions:

1. In the Crockpot, combine chicken thighs, barbecue sauce, soy sauce, honey, garlic, and ginger.

2. Cover and cook on low for four-six hours, or until the chicken is tender.

3. Serve the chicken garnished with sliced green onions and sesame seeds.

Duration for this recipe: four-six hours on low
Nutrients (per portion, without garnishes):
- Caloric content: 280
- Amino content: 25g
- Carb content: 20g
- Fatty acid: 10g

4. FUSION PORK CURRY

Ingredients:
- two lbs pork shoulder, cubed
- one onion, chopped
- two cloves garlic, minced
- two tablespoonful curry powder
- one can (fourteen oz) coconut milk
- one cupful chicken broth
- two carrots, sliced
- one bell pepper, chopped
- Salt and black pepper to taste
- Chopped fresh cilantro (for garnish)

Instructions:

1. In the Crockpot, combine cubed pork shoulder, chopped onion, minced garlic, curry powder, coconut milk, chicken broth, sliced carrots, chopped bell pepper, salt, and black pepper.

2. Cover and cook on low for six-eight hours.

3. Serve the pork curry garnished with chopped fresh cilantro.

Duration for this recipe: six-eight hours on low
Nutrients (per portion, without garnish):
- Caloric content: 320
- Amino content: 24g
- Carb content: 10g
- Fatty acid: 21g

5. CRISPY CHINESE SHREDDED CHICKEN

Ingredients:
- two lbs boneless chicken breasts
- half cupful soy sauce
- one-fourth cupful hoisin sauce
- one-fourth cupful honey
- two cloves garlic, minced
- one teaspoonful ginger, minced
- one-fourth cupful cornstarch
- Sliced green onions (for garnish)
- Sesame seeds (for garnish)

Instructions:

1. In the Crockpot, combine chicken breasts, soy sauce, hoisin sauce, honey, garlic, and ginger.

2. Cover and cook on low for four-six hours, or until the chicken is tender.

3. Remove the chicken from the Crockpot and shred it.

4. In a skillet, heat the sauce from the Crockpot and whisk in cornstarch to thicken.

5. Toss the shredded chicken in the thickened sauce.

6. Serve the shredded chicken garnished with sliced green onions and sesame seeds.

Duration for this recipe: four-six hours on low
Nutrients (per portion, without garnishes):
- Caloric content: 260
- Amino content: 25g
- Carb content: 20g
- Fatty acid: 7g

6. KIMCHI STEW WITH BEEF

Ingredients:
- one lb beef stew meat
- two cupful kimchi, chopped
- one onion, chopped
- two cloves garlic, minced
- one tablespoonful gochugaru (Korean red pepper flakes)
- one tablespoonful gochujang (Korean red pepper paste)
- four cupful beef broth
- one cupful water
- one cupful tofu, cubed
- two green onions, chopped
- Cooked rice (for serving)

Instructions:

1. In the Crockpot, combine beef stew meat, chopped kimchi, chopped onion, minced garlic, gochugaru, gochujang, beef broth, and water.

2. Cover and cook on low for six-eight hours.

3. Stir in tofu and let it cook for an additional 30 minutes.

4. Serve the kimchi stew with chopped green onions over cooked rice.

Duration for this recipe: six-eight hours on low
Nutrients (per portion, excluding rice):
- Caloric content: 260

- Amino content: 25g
- Carb content: 10g
- Fatty acid: 15g

7. KOREAN SLOPPY JOE

Ingredients:
- one lb ground beef
- one onion, chopped
- two cloves garlic, minced
- one-fourth cupful gochujang (Korean red pepper paste)
- one-fourth cupful soy sauce
- one-fourth cupful ketchup
- two tablespoonful brown sugar
- Sliced green onions (for garnish)
- Hamburger buns

Instructions:

1. In a skillet, brown the ground beef and drain excess fat.

2. In the Crockpot, combine the browned beef, chopped onion, minced garlic, gochujang, soy sauce, ketchup, and brown sugar.

3. Cover and cook on low for four-six hours.

4. Serve the Korean sloppy joe on hamburger buns, garnished with sliced green onions.

Duration for this recipe: four-six hours on low
Nutrients (per portion, without bun and garnish):
- Caloric content: 260
- Amino content: 20g
- Carb content: 12g
- Fatty acid: 14g

8. CHICKEN CURRY WITH YUKON GOLD POTATOES

Ingredients:
- two lbs boneless chicken thighs
- four Yukon Gold potatoes, peeled and cubed
- one onion, chopped
- two cloves garlic, minced
- two tablespoonful curry powder
- one can (fourteen oz) diced tomatoes
- one can (fourteen oz) coconut milk

- one cupful chicken broth
- Salt and black pepper to taste
- Chopped fresh cilantro (for garnish)

Instructions:

1. In the Crockpot, combine chicken thighs, cubed Yukon Gold potatoes, chopped onion, minced garlic, curry powder, diced tomatoes, coconut milk, chicken broth, salt, and black pepper.

2. Cover and cook on low for six-eight hours.

3. Serve the chicken curry garnished with chopped fresh cilantro.

Duration for this recipe: six-eight hours on low
Nutrients (per portion, without garnish):

- Caloric content: 350
- Amino content: 25g
- Carb content: 20g
- Fatty acid: 20g

9. KALBI BEEF POUTINE

Ingredients:

- two lbs beef short ribs, cut into pieces
- one cupful Korean BBQ sauce (Kalbi marinade)
- one cupful shredded mozzarella cheese
- half cupful beef gravy
- French fries
- Sliced green onions (for garnish)

Instructions:

1. In the Crockpot, combine beef short ribs and Korean BBQ sauce.

2. Cover and cook on low for six-eight hours.

3. Serve the Kalbi beef over French fries, topped with shredded mozzarella cheese and beef gravy.

4. Garnish with sliced green onions.

Duration for this recipe: six-eight hours on low
Nutrients (per portion, without fries and garnishes):

- Caloric content: 300
- Amino content: 20g
- Carb content: 15g
- Fatty acid: 18g

10. MOROCCAN CHICKPEA STEW

Ingredients:

- two cans (fourteen oz each) chickpeas, drained and rinsed
- one onion, chopped
- two cloves garlic, minced
- two carrots, chopped
- two tomatoes, chopped
- two cupful vegetable broth
- one teaspoonful ground cumin
- one teaspoonful ground coriander
- half teaspoonful ground cinnamon
- one-fourth teaspoonful cayenne pepper (adjust to taste)
- Salt and black pepper to taste
- Chopped fresh cilantro (for garnish)

Instructions:

1. In the Crockpot, combine chickpeas, chopped onion, minced garlic, chopped carrots, chopped tomatoes, vegetable broth, ground cumin, ground coriander, ground cinnamon, cayenne pepper, salt, and black pepper.

2. Cover and cook on low for six-eight hours.

3. Serve the Moroccan chickpea stew garnished with chopped fresh cilantro.

Duration for this recipe: six-eight hours on low
Nutrients (per portion, excluding garnish):

- Caloric content: 250
- Amino content: 10g
- Carb content: 45g
- Fatty acid: 3g

11. ITALIAN WEDDING SOUP

Ingredients:

- one lb ground Italian sausage
- one onion, chopped
- two carrots, chopped
- two celery stalks, chopped
- three cloves garlic, minced
- six cupful chicken broth
- two cupful spinach, chopped
- half cupful orzo pasta
- one-fourth cupful grated Parmesan cheese

- Salt and black pepper to taste

Instructions:

1. In a skillet, brown the Italian sausage and drain excess fat.

2. In the Crockpot, combine browned Italian sausage, chopped onion, chopped carrots, chopped celery, minced garlic, chicken broth, and orzo pasta.

3. Cover and cook on low for four-six hours.

4. Stir in chopped spinach and grated Parmesan cheese.

5. Season with salt and black pepper to taste.

Duration for this recipe: four-six hours on low

Nutrients (per portion, excluding salt and pepper):

- Caloric content: 280
- Amino content: 18g
- Carb content: 20g
- Fatty acid: 14g

12. MEXICAN POZOLE

Ingredients:

- one lb pork shoulder, cubed
- one onion, chopped
- two cloves garlic, minced
- two cans (fifteen oz each) hominy, drained and rinsed
- four cupful chicken broth
- two teaspoonful ground cumin
- two teaspoonful chili powder
- Salt and black pepper to taste
- Chopped fresh cilantro (for garnish)
- Lime wedges (for serving)

Instructions:

1. In the Crockpot, combine cubed pork shoulder, chopped onion, minced garlic, hominy, chicken broth, ground cumin, chili powder, salt, and black pepper.

2. Cover and cook on low for six-eight hours.

3. Serve the Mexican pozole garnished with chopped fresh cilantro and lime wedges.

Duration for this recipe: six-eight hours on low

Nutrients (per portion, excluding garnish):

- Caloric content: 280
- Amino content: 20g
- Carb content: 20g
- Fatty acid: 14g

13. THAI RED CURRY CHICKEN

Ingredients:

- two lbs boneless chicken thighs, cut into pieces
- one can (fourteen oz) coconut milk
- two tablespoonful red curry paste
- one red bell pepper, chopped
- one zucchini, chopped
- one onion, chopped
- two cloves garlic, minced
- one tablespoonful fish sauce
- one tablespoonful brown sugar
- one lime, juiced
- Fresh cilantro and basil (for garnish)
- Cooked rice (for serving)

Instructions:

1. In the Crockpot, combine chicken thighs, coconut milk, red curry paste, chopped red bell pepper, chopped zucchini, chopped onion, minced garlic, fish sauce, and brown sugar.

2. Cover and cook on low for four-six hours.

3. Stir in fresh lime juice.

4. Serve the Thai red curry chicken over cooked rice, garnished with fresh cilantro and basil.

Duration for this recipe: four-six hours on low

*Nutrients (per portion, without rice and garnish):

- Caloric content: 200
- Amino content: 10g
- Carb content: 17g
- Fatty acid: 12g

ALPHABETICAL INDEX

Made in the USA
Monee, IL
17 May 2024

58574481R00052